fun excuses to talk about God

by
Joani Schultz

Group
Loveland, Colorado

*To my son, Matt, and my husband, Thom, who are
two of God's greatest excuses for me to give thanks!
I love you two!*

fun excuses to talk about God

Copyright © 1997 Joani Schultz

Credits

Editor: Bob Buller
Managing Editor: Michael D. Warden
Copy Editor: Janis Sampson
Art Director: Lisa Chandler
Cover Art Director: Helen H. Lannis
Computer Graphic Artist: Joyce Douglas
Cover Designer: Diana Walters
Cover Illustrator: Stacey Lamb
Illustrator: Beth Roberge
Production Manager: Gingar Kunkel

Unless otherwise noted, Scriptures quoted from The Youth Bible, New
Century Version, copyright © 1991 by Word Publishing, Dallas, Texas
75039. Used by permission.

Library of Congress Cataloging-in-Publication Data
Schultz, Joani, 1953-
    Fun excuses to talk about God / by Joani Schultz.
      p.   cm.
    Includes index.
    ISBN 0-7644-2012-7
    1. Family--Prayer-books and devotions--English. 2. Family-
  -Religious aspects--Christianity.   I. Title.
    BV255.S37   1997
    249--dc21
                                              97-3396
                                                CIP

10 9 8 7 6 5 4 3 2   06 05 04 03 02 01 00 99 98 97
Printed in the United States of America.

contents

introduction

Your faith and Christian values must be important to you and your family. You've picked up this book. You've gotten this far. And that's good!

But if you're like most people, having family devotions is a struggle. It's the "right answer," what you're supposed to do. But all too often your busy family schedule crowds out family devotions, and it becomes one more thing to feel guilty about.

If this is your situation, let Fun Excuses to Talk About God be the start of an entirely new approach to family devotions. It's worked in our family, and I know it can work in yours! Fun Excuses to Talk About God shows you how to make spending time with God something your family will actually look forward to.

This book presents a fun, practical, and easy way to create "excuses" for weaving your faith and values into your day-to-day lives. By sharing family stories, making memories through simple activities, reading and discussing Scripture, and praying, you'll make your faith a part of your everyday lives. And isn't that what Jesus was hoping for in the first place? Jesus doesn't want us to stick him neatly into a ten-minute time slot once a week. I believe Jesus wants us to see him at every turn, at any time—no matter where we are or who we're with. Wouldn't it be great if we could create excuses to talk about how God is at work in our lives all the time?

That's the concept behind Fun Excuses to Talk About God! Here's how it works:

It's FUN because...

• YOU'LL FIND FUN IDEAS FOR UNFORGETTABLE ACTIVITIES IN EACH DEVOTION. Imagine using a set of keys to remind your family that Jesus opens our way to God or a piece of rope to learn about heaven. Creative experiences like these helped our family remember God's Word and have fun, and they will do the same for your family!

• YOU WON'T HAVE TO SPEND TIME PLANNING OR PREPARING THE DEVOTION. Many parents feel intimidated to "lead" family devotions. But that's not a problem with Fun Excuses to Talk About God! These devotions are focused on learners (not leaders!) and involve everyone. In addition, all you'll need to do in most cases is to grab a simple prop such as toilet paper, a spoon, or a pencil and then watch as your children eagerly help make the devotion happen. I loved seeing my son, Matt, leap from his chair to round up the devotional prop—and then talk about how Jesus is active in his young life. And he enjoyed hearing Thom and I tell how Jesus is important to us as adults.

- **YOU'LL USE JESUS' METHODS OF TEACHING.** Our Lord was notorious for using common objects of his day to relate powerful truths that amazed and profoundly affected his listeners. Who would ever forget the lessons learned from the mustard seed, the net, the coins, the fig tree, or the basin and towel? In the same way, when you use objects you see and use every day to teach a biblical truth, you and your family will remember that lesson for a long time.

It's EXCUSES TO TALK because...

- **EACH DEVOTION IS LOADED WITH "EXCUSES" TO TALK ABOUT GOD AND HOW HE IS ACTIVE IN OUR EVERYDAY LIVES.** These conversation sparks will get your family talking—about God, about life, even about what happened at school or work during the day. As a result, family members will learn more about each other and about God's love for them. A love like that makes each day worth living! And the more excuses and reasons to talk about God's love, the better!

- **YOU'LL ENJOY TELLING YOUR OWN "FAMILY STORIES."** Each devotion begins with storytelling. Both Thom and I grew up in families that love to talk and tell stories! Consequently, we've both learned the value of talking things out. We talk about everything—the news, how the day went, the latest project at work, the goofy thing that happened to us after church, Matt's latest interest. Everything. Through the process of storytelling, our faith stories get mingled together with our life stories. Families who talk about their faith with each other generally have vibrant personal relationships with God. It really works! So each devotion makes sure that you'll have something to talk about.

It's ABOUT GOD because...

- **YOU'LL USE THE BIBLE AS A RELEVANT GUIDE FOR YOU AND YOUR FAMILY.** Each devotion includes a Scripture passage to spark discussion about how God is alive and active in your lives today. You'll give your children the best gift of all—a solid grounding in God's Word!

• **EACH DEVOTION USES AN EVERYDAY OBJECT TO REINFORCE WHAT YOU LEARNED ABOUT GOD DURING THE WEEK.** For example, you'll become detectives looking for a cross wherever you can spy one, or you'll use a ring to remind you of God's promises, or you'll think about prayer when the telephone rings. Our Lord is present everywhere, so these devotions help family members of all ages be on the lookout for God's presence in our lives.

• **PRAYER FORMS A SPECIAL PART OF EACH DEVOTION.** Because the prayers are participatory, everyone will get a chance to talk to God. These prayers allow family members an opportunity to pray for one another in meaningful ways that will bring them closer to God and to each other.

God gave us families to help us grow. Families are labs in which we learn and live out our Christian faith and values. Parents bring experience, knowledge, and wisdom; while kids contribute questions, curiosity, and a refreshing sense of wonder. When parents and kids talk and listen to each other, their relationships grow. So use *Fun Excuses to Talk About God* to grow closer as a family *and* to deepen your faith in God. And while you do, keep in mind these final tips.

Ten Quick Tips for Using This Book

1. **USE A FAMILY-FRIENDLY BIBLE.** In plain language, use a Bible that uses plain language. Nothing is more frustrating for kids than to stumble over a Bible translation that's way over their heads. So use the New International Version, the International Children's Bible, Today's English Version, or the New Century Version. Any of these versions presents God's Word in easy-to-understand-and-apply language.

2. **RESPECT EACH PERSON.** Each family member is valuable, precious, and irreplaceable. No matter what a person's age or what he or she might say, each person has the right to be respected. When one person talks, everyone else listens. Everyone gets a turn. No insults, interruptions, or ignoring. In short, every family member gives the

other family members the respect he or she wants in return.

3. TALK ABOUT ANY SUBJECT. If something is important enough for one family member to bring up, it's important for others to talk about. The "no taboo" rule also goes for tough subjects such as cheating, alcohol abuse, bad language, sex, or hitting. You'll know that a subject is tough for your family when it's something you're nervous about bringing up. The more nervous you are, the more important it is to talk about it.

4. BE THANKFUL FOR EACH OTHER. Always look for reasons (and ways) to appreciate each other. The trouble is, when we live with people day in and day out, we see the best and worst of each other. Too often we dwell on what bugs us instead of what we're thankful for. When we focus on the joys instead of jabs, we discover what we really do love about each other. And we see that we wouldn't be the special family we are without each valuable person.

5. LAUGH A LOT. Look for the funny stuff around you. Philippians says, "Rejoice in the Lord always," so we need to hunt for the joy that God brings us through our family members. If you can find even a twinge of humor in the heat of a family battle, it will help soften the tough stuff.

6. DON'T BE AFRAID OF "I DON'T KNOW." Kids ask a lot of questions, and that's great. But sometimes we adults have a hard time admitting we don't know everything. Who knows, your child may need to hear a long-overdue admission of those three little words, "I don't know." Then work together to find books or people who can help you when your family gets stumped. And don't leave the answer-getting to the adults. Assign different family members to research and find out any information you're lacking.

7. CREATE FAMILY TRADITIONS. You can do these devotions whenever you'd like, but it might make life easier to set aside a special time— maybe after breakfast or before bedtime. Or you might be the type of family that sets one night a week as a sacred family time. However you do it, remember that one of the traits of healthy families is that they have traditions—special times to celebrate and cement family bonds.

8. MAKE FAMILY TIME "TALK TIME." Show everyone that you want to listen by turning off the television and putting away the newspaper!

Let the phone answering machine do its job. To reinforce the message that this is family time, light candles at the dinner table or have hot chocolate before bed. Make your family time a special time. Think about the years to come. Your children will recall these special moments far longer than some television rerun. You're making memories.

9. USE THIS BOOK IN ANY WAY YOU'D LIKE. Go in order from start to finish or pick and choose according to the topic that strikes your fancy each week. You may even want to photocopy the table of contents and create slips with one devotion on each slip. Then place the slips in a cookie jar, a coffee can, or a kid-decorated basket; take turns pulling out a new devotion topic each week. Be ready for some surprises!

10. TAKE TURNS LEADING THE DEVOTIONS. Any family member (who can read) can guide your family members through your devotion time. For fun, allow different family members to take the lead. It's more fun for Mom or Dad to have kids take ownership of the devotions than to feel as though they have to nag everyone else into participating. And after a few devotions, you'll discover that no one wants to miss this time of together-talking and family fun. In fact, our son, Matt, soon became the one to say, "Let's do our devotions now!" It was heartwarming to see Matt eager to dig into God's Word. It's a feeling that I pray you will enjoy as you take advantage of all these *Fun Excuses to Talk About God!*

Jesus is the key

TALK TOPIC: *Jesus*

Our Family Stories

It seems as though we can't get anywhere without keys these days. Keys start cars, open doors, unlock suitcases and safes. As a family, list all the times and places you need keys. Then talk about why keys are so important. You might even discuss what happened when people you know misplaced or lost their keys.

Today's Memory Maker

Grab a set of keys right now. Dangle and jingle them to see how they sound. For the next few moments, play the Key Match Game. The "key dangler" points one of the keys toward a family member. Then that family member guesses what that particular key opens. To check how "key smart" your family is, have each key dangler see if the key actually fits the lock the other person guessed.

Once you've had a little fun, have each person tell about a time he or she *really* needed keys. (Even toddlers know that keys get them into the car or house!) Did you have to get into someplace impor- tant—fast? Have you ever been locked out of your car or home? What's happened that has made you glad for keys?

Today's Bible Insight

Now look up John 14:6 in the Bible. Then have someone use one key to point to each word in the verse while some- one else reads it. You'll discover that Jesus said some important words about who he is.

Hmm…it sounds as

though Jesus is describing himself as the key to God. Take a moment to discuss the following questions:

- How is Jesus like a key to open the way to God? How is he different?
- What would happen if we didn't have Jesus as our key to get to God?
- How has Jesus helped us in important times—just as our keys have helped us?

Our Family Prayers

Place the set of keys in front of you. Then take turns saying a prayer sentence for every key. The number of keys you carry on the set will determine the number of prayers. Your prayers can include a prayer for Jesus' help with something, a prayer thanking God for sending Jesus, or a prayer for someone else you're concerned about. (You may never look at your key ring the same again!)

During the Week

Every time you see or reach for a key…

- thank God that Jesus is the only key that opens the way to God and to heaven.
- think of someone you know who might not have the key— Jesus. Then decide how you can tell him or her about Jesus. You could become a key witness to that person knowing Jesus as the key to God!

To make sure that you're ready to tell others about Jesus, every time you use a key, repeat John 14:6 together.

family bloopers

TALK TOPIC: *Mistakes*

Our Family Stories

Yikes! Who hasn't blown it and messed up? We hate to admit it, but the truth is, we *all* make mistakes. So take a deep breath, and tell each other about a time you made a mistake. Was it when you forgot someone's birthday or didn't do what you promised? Whatever it is, honestly admit it and tell each other what happened. Everybody listens, and no snide comments allowed!

Today's Memory Maker

Now grab a pencil with an eraser and a sheet of scrap paper. (The bigger the better!) Then take turns telling how you felt when you realized your blooper. Did you feel silly? embarrassed? ashamed? something else? As each person explains, he or she must scribble on the paper some word or picture that represents those feelings. By the way, have each person scribble on top of the other scribbles. You want to make a nice, big mess.

Today's Bible Insight

Next, take out your Bible, and read the first half of Romans 8:28. Then, to see how this promise might work, have a volunteer use the eraser to erase a giant outline of a heart in the middle of the scribbles. Bloopers be gone!

Then discuss the following questions:

• How does the heart in the middle of the scribbles make our bloopers look now?

• How is that like God turning the bad stuff in our lives into something good?

Think about each of your mistakes. Help each other think of what you learned (or can learn) from your mistakes. Try to discover how God might use your bloopers and what you learned from your bloopers for good. If you have time, talk about other mistakes you've made recently and what you can learn from them.

Our Family Prayers

Now it's time to thank God for his goodness. One by one, tell God why you're thankful for his perfect promise in Romans 8:28a. Then have another volunteer erase each family member's initials inside the heart on the scribble page as you pray: "Thank you, Lord, for (name) because..."

During the Week

Every time you see or use a pencil and eraser this week...

• remember that God loves you and wants to turn your bad bloopers into something super.

• tell a friend why it's sometimes hard to believe that God can turn our mistakes into something good.

For extra fun, whenever one family member hands another a pencil and points to the eraser, they must say Romans 8:28a together.

---

i know you!

TALK TOPIC: *Loving each other*

Our Family Stories

It's easier to love people—including other family members—when we know and understand them. So here's a way to really get to know each other.

Take a few minutes to interview each other. Start by interviewing the oldest family member, then the youngest, then the next to the oldest, and so on. Ask about anything you'd like to know more about. This is your chance to be investigative reporters! You can make up your own questions or try some of the following:

• **What did you do today? What did you think about during the day?**

• Who did you spend most of your time with during the day? Why?

• What was the best part of your day? the worst part of your day?

• If you could've done something else today, what would it have been?

(If you use this devotion at breakfast time, ask each other about the day before.)

Today's Memory Maker

Now, for added fun, switch roles. For example, kids can become parents and parents become kids. Take a minute to decide who will be who. The only rule is you can't be yourself! (You can choose to switch roles for a mealtime—or for as long as you'd like!)

For however long you choose, everyone must talk, act, and think like the family member assigned to him or her. Have fun! Enjoy a few laughs. Just *don't* be yourself!

After you've taken time to be someone else, discuss what you learned about the person you were playing: How easy was it to be that person? What makes it hard to understand someone else? How well do you *really* know each other?

Today's Bible Insight

Read 1 John 4:20-21, which teaches us about loving each other. Then discuss the following questions:

• Why is it important for us to love each other?

• What makes it hard to love each other all the time?

• How will understanding others help us love them more?

Take turns describing one way you can be more understanding of each other and one way you can be more loving toward each other. Then take a few minutes to tell how each person is important and valuable to the family.

Our Family Prayers

When you're finished talking about your love for one another, *show* each other love. Have a fun family hug with everybody huddling together for a close "lovebug hug." Then while you're still in your lovebug hug, have each person say a short prayer thanking the God of love for the love in your family.

During the Week

Whenever you see or hear a news reporter…
- turn to a family member and ask a specific question about his or her day.
- switch roles with the family member nearest you for the next fifteen minutes.

Whenever things get tense, say together 1 John 4:21, "And God gave us this command: Those who love God must also love their brothers and sisters."

being a "God" example

TALK TOPIC: *Loving others*

Our Family Stories

Have you ever heard someone say, "You're the spittin' image of your mom (or dad)"? People say that when they think you look a lot like someone else. Have each person tell about a time someone said he or she looked just like someone else. Go ahead—tell all the silly, embarrassing, or even feel-good details. Talk about how it feels when people say those things about you.

Today's Memory Maker

Genesis 1:26 says that we've been created in the spittin' image of God. Since God doesn't have a body, we can't *look* like him. So how can we be made in his image? Well...there *is* a fun way to be in someone else's image. Think of a mirror.

For the next few moments, your family members will become human mirrors. Form pairs. (If there's an uneven number in your family, you can form a trio and become one of those fancy bifold mirrors!) Face each other, and pretend you're looking in the mirror. Have the youngest partner in each pair be the leader. Whatever actions the youngest partner makes, the older one must follow just like a mirror image. After a few moments, trade places.

Now tell each other what it was like to be the mirror image. When was it easy? What made it hard?

Today's Bible Insight

Since we've been created in God's image, how should we act? Open your Bible, and read 1 Peter 2:12b for the answer.

Everything you say or do is a reflection of God's image to others. What you say or do shows other people what God is like. How does it feel to know that what you say and do reflects God to others? If you treat each other kindly, what does that say about God? If you fight, what does that tell others about God?

Think of your family as a mirror reflecting God's love to others. Have each person describe what other people see your family doing. For example, how do you spend your time? If people peeked into your daily routine, what would it tell them? When your family members talk, what would people learn about God? When do others see God's love in your family? When do they not see God's love?

Then have family members each name one person to whom they can show God's love. They might think of people at work, at school, in the neighborhood—or even another family member. Take turns telling about that person, what you'll do to show love, and what that person will think about God after you're through.

Our Family Prayers

Now join hands, and say a prayer of thanks to God for making all of you in his image. Then say a prayer of thanks for each family member and how you've each seen that person reflect God's love to someone. Be specific and encouraging. Finally have the oldest family member close with a prayer for God's help to live in a way that honors him.

During the Week

Every time you see or look in a mirror...

• say, "Thanks, God, for using me as a good example!" or "Help, God, it's hard to reflect your image."

• teach a friend the Mirror Game. Then use it to tell that friend about God's love.

Several times during the week, ask a family member to play the Mirror Game again. As you play, say 1 Peter 2:12b together.

top ten joy bringers

TALK TOPIC: *Joy*

Our Family Stories

David Letterman made Top Ten lists famous. But since he hasn't made a Top Ten list for *your* family, it's up to you! Have your family members put together your very own unique-to-your-family Top Ten list. Here's how.

For starters, divide your family into two groups. Since this devotion will require some writing, pair younger children with parents or older kids. (If you have three or fewer in your family, work together as one group.) Then have each group pick a different topic to work on. Groups can choose from the following list of topics or create their own categories: favorite places to go on a family vacation, favorite family memories, favorite places to live, favorite rooms in the house, favorite TV programs, or favorite foods.

Today's Memory Maker

Now the real fun begins! Give each group a sheet of paper and a pencil. Have each group work separately to write its list—that's so it can be a surprise to the other group!

Allow a few minutes of "think time" to create your Top Ten lists. If some family members want to draw their ideas, instead of write them, that's fine. Once the master lists have been completed, take turns revealing what you wrote to the other half of the family. Start with the number ten item on the list, elaborating on the answers. For a fun twist, try to *guess* what the other group listed for its category before it reveals its answers.

Now compare each other's lists. Talk about what surprised you. What was the most unexpected answer? the least surprising one? How might the answers differ if the groups exchanged lists?

Today's Bible Insight

Now read Philippians 4:4.

The truth is, God gives us more than ten things to be glad about when it comes to our families. So right now, starting with number ten, have each person contribute to a countdown of ten things you're glad that God has done for you and your family. Think of what God has given that brings you joy. Have the youngest family member hold up ten fingers and then put one finger down as you call out those things. Ready? Ten...

Did you list ten? Now discuss the following questions:
• How easy was it to list ten things to be glad about?
• How can we show our joy for what God has given our family?

Our Family Prayers

In a fun sort of way, you've just prayed and rejoiced to God with your Top Ten list. Now huddle close. Instead of joining hands, have each person hold up his or her fingers, crisscross thumbs, and join with the other family members' pinkies. Look at those ten fingers each person has. Use your hands as reminders this week of God's Top Ten joy bringers to your family. To close, have each person say a one-sentence, eye-open prayer of thanks and joy.

During the Week

Every time you get a chance, give each other a "high ten"—slapping both palms together with someone else. Then...

- complete the sentence, "I'm glad God put you in our family because…"
- think up other top ten categories to learn more about each other.

For extra fun, give a high ten as one family member says, "Rejoice in the Lord always." Then have the other family member say, "And again I say, rejoice!" It'll be a fun way to remember God's Word together.

no room for love

TALK TOPIC: *Judging others*

Our Family Stories

We all can think of people who bug us. And before you know it, we're bad-mouthing them, saying nasty things to others about what bugs us. Maybe we call the neighbors names because of the way they keep their yard or make fun of how someone looks, acts, or talks. When we pick on stuff about other people, it's called judging.

Have each person tell why they get bugged by someone else, whether that person is a family member or someone outside the family. Use this as a time to honestly confess when you may have judged someone unfairly.

Today's Memory Maker

Now fill a glass or small bowl to the brim with water. Imagine that the water is love. Look at how full the glass is! Now give each person an egg or other solid object that will displace the water. Have family members each tell what bugs them about other people as they place the egg into the water.

Watch what happens to the water in the glass. Is there room for both the water and the egg? Why or why not? How is this similar to what happens when we spend our time judging people rather than loving them?

Now take a moment to examine your own family. What things do you as a family judge other people about? Do you judge people who make different choices than you would make? Are you jealous of others who have more things or get better grades than you do? Or what about people who dress differently? who are a different color? who follow a different religion?

Today's Bible Insight

God knows us really well. And he knows we're often tempted to judge others. But that's dangerous business. Open your Bible to Matthew 7:1-5, and think about your water experiment as a volunteer reads the verses.

Then discuss the following questions:
- Why is it tempting for us to judge others?
- Why does God not want us to judge others?
- What does God want us to do instead of judging others?

Pause for a moment and have each person silently think of someone he or she has judged in the past. After you've all thought of someone, take turns telling what you can do to change your judgmental attitudes into loving actions.

Our Family Prayers

Have each person carefully hold an egg (or the object used earlier). One by one, say a prayer of confession for a time you've been guilty of judging someone. Close your prayer by thanking God for his forgiveness and asking him to help your family be more loving and less judgmental.

Use the eggs to symbolize your commitment to stop judging others and to start loving them. You can celebrate with scrambled eggs or omelets for the next meal. Eating your eggs can be one more reminder as you swallow and digest this lesson!

During the Week

Every time you drink a glass of water or see an egg…

• think of one thing you can do to show love to someone whom you're tempted to judge. Then follow through with your loving action.

• say a silent prayer thanking God for his forgiveness and asking him to help you be more loving and less judging.

For extra fun, pour a glass of water for someone as you say Matthew 7:1 together. The trick will be to pour the water so it takes exactly as much time to fill the glass as it takes to say the verse!

what's in a name?

TALK TOPIC: *Communication*

Our Family Stories

There's real power in our names. We all know how important it is to have our names pronounced and spelled correctly. And we all know how special we feel when people remember our names.

Take a few minutes to tell stories about your names. Parents, explain why you decided to name your children what you did. Is anyone named after a relative or famous person? Then have everyone talk about his or her name. Do you have any funny stories about your name? How do you feel about your name and why? Do you have a nickname that you like or hate? If you had the power to rename yourself, what would you choose as your name and why?

Today's Memory Maker

Have each family member write his or her name on a small slip of paper and then fold it up and plunk it into a dish. Then have each person draw out a name (other than his or her own) and say it in one of the following ways. The person reading the name gets to choose how to say it!

—Whisper it. —Cry it.
—Shout it. —Laugh it.
—Whine it. —Tease it.

After family members hear their names, have them tell how hearing their names said that way made them feel. When everyone's name has been read, talk about times family members have said each other's names in these ways. How did you feel when that happened? Are there other ways people say your name that you like—or hate?

Today's Bible Insight

Our names aren't just important to us—they're also important to God. Read John 10:2-3 to find out just how important they are. Then discuss the following questions:

• How does it feel to know that Jesus knows your name?
• What would it be like if Jesus didn't know your name?
• How do you think Jesus "says" your name? Explain.

Now each of you think of a way you can be more like Jesus when you use each other's names. Tell how you'll use people's names differently. For example, instead of being irritated and whining, "Maaaaaatt!" when Mom wants Matt to stop slurping his soup—Mom may need to gently say, "Matt, sipping your soup quietly will show us your good manners."

Our Family Prayers

Join hands. Pause for a few moments while family members think about hurtful ways they've said each other's names in the past and helpful ways they will say them in the future. Then go around the circle and have family members each thank God for calling them by name and ask God to help them say each other's names as Jesus would.

Every time you see your name or one of your family member's names...
- tell two things you really like about that name.
- grab the family member nearest you, and recite together the verse that tells you Jesus calls you by name, John 10:3.

For extra fun, find a book that tells you what different names mean and look up family members' and friends' names!

don't touch that remote!

TALK TOPIC: *Television*

Our Family Stories

Ssshhhh! My favorite show is coming on! Hey! Don't touch that remote! I'm watching this!

What are your family's television-viewing habits? Tell each other why you like your favorite television programs. Explain why watching television is or is not important to you. Describe how you'd feel if someone robbed your home and took the television set (or sets). How would your daily life be different if the television disappeared? (Maybe someone in the family remembers what life was like before the invention of television. Tell what that was like!)

Today's Memory Maker

Now gather in front of your family's television. Turn it on. For a few moments, have the youngest family member play with the channels and volume. Then have that person turn up the volume to a level that makes it hard to hear each other.

Then, beginning with the youngest person, have everyone tell about the best thing that happened that day (or the day before, if you're meeting at breakfast). After everyone's had a chance to share, turn off the TV. Discuss what it was like to talk over the sound or to "tune into" the person talking. How is this like the way television drowns out family conversation at other times? How is it different?

The rest of this memory maker depends on your family having a good imagination—and determination. Here's the challenge for the next day, few days, or more—you choose the time frame. Pretend your television set is broken. That means no more television for anyone—adults included! You can unplug your television(s) for this time or even deputize guards to keep family members from sneaking a peek! Make this a family adventure!

Since your television is out of commission—now what? Talk about what you'll do instead. What could you do together that you otherwise wouldn't have time to do? How can you take advantage of "NO TV"?

Today's Bible Insight

Maybe you need some help deciding what to do with your time now that television is out of the question. How can you tell what God wants with your time—with or without television? Take a look at Philippians 4:8. It even uses family words.

Now talk about your family's activities and how they stack up against each key word in Philippians 4:8. Use the following chart to help you decide how your family can obey Paul's command.

Putting Philippians 4:8 Into Practice

Things we can do together that are...	With TV	Without TV
good		
worthy of praise		
true		
honorable		
right		
pure		
beautiful		
respected		

Our Family Prayers

Gather near the television for a farewell ceremony. Join in a family circle, and say a prayer for strength and patience to go without the television. Ask God to make your family bonds stronger as you concentrate on doing positive activities together as a family.

As a reminder of your commitment not to watch television, tape a piece of newspaper over the screen or write, "Do not remove until (the date you chose)" on a sheet of paper, and tape it to the television.

During the Week

Every time you see a television screen...

• talk to someone in your family—about anything at all! Simply talk together!

• have your entire family do one of the "Without TV" activities you listed on the "Putting Philippians 4:8 Into Practice" chart (p. 26).

To remember all the key words from Philippians 4:8, concentrate on one word each day of the week. For example, think about "good" things you can do together on Sunday, things that are "worthy of praise" on Monday, and so on. If you do two words on the seventh day, you'll have memorized the entire verse by the end of the week.

TALK TOPIC: *Thankfulness*

Our Family Stories

Memories. That's what cements a family together. Every family has its own special blend of stories and experiences that makes it unique. Bask in a few memories right now. Let each person finish this sentence: "When I think of our family, I remember when..."

You can recall any kind of memory—serious, silly, scary, significant, or whatever. For example, our family might remember when we biked to the theater but couldn't make it all the way home because we were too pooped to peddle back up the hill. Or we might remember when we traveled to South Dakota for Great-Grandma's funeral. Continue for as long as you'd like.

Today's Memory Maker

This memory maker is up to you. Brainstorm together what item or symbol best represents your family memories. Maybe you'll choose a picture on the wall, a refrigerator magnet, or even an old sock! As a family, decide what will be a unique reminder of your family. Just think—it's possible no other family would choose the same item. Your family memories are what help make you so special!

Once you've selected your family memory maker, have each person tell why it's such a good representation of your family memories. Then talk about what life would be like if we were unable to remember people, places, or experiences.

Today's Bible Insight

"Remembering" holds a special place in our Christian heritage. We love to recall and retell God's story of love in our lives. It's also important to remember special people who have shown love to us. Read Philippians 1:3-6 to find out how important the apostle Paul's memories were to him. Then take a few minutes to discuss the following questions:

• Which of these words or phrases could we use about our family? Explain.

• Which words or phrases wouldn't we use? Why wouldn't we use them?

• When are you thankful for your family's help? When do you need more help?

• How can we follow Paul's example of giving thanks for our family members?

Our Family Prayers

This will be a fill-in-the-blank prayer. Here's how it works. Have each person complete the three sentences below for each family member. (If some family members haven't learned to read yet, have someone else read each sentence so they can repeat it.)

—I thank God every time I remember (name).

—I thank God for the help (name) gave me when (tell about a time that person helped you).

—I know God is doing a good work in (name) because (tell how that person does good for the family).

Close with a prayer thanking God for the special memories your family shares and asking God to remind you to be thankful for each other.

During the Week

Every time you see your family memory maker...

• point it out to each family member and say, "I'm really thankful for you because..."

• brainstorm ideas to create future memories together. For example, you might plan a picnic, choose a family game night, or even talk about a family vacation.

To remind you to be thankful for each other, recite Philippians 1:3-4 every time a family member uses the word "remember."

the juggling family

TALK TOPIC: *Busyness*

Our Family Stories

Life is so crazy these days that sometimes families seem like bumper cars at an amusement park. Family members go their own ways, occasionally bumping into each other on purpose but all too often getting blindsided by unexpected people or unforeseen problems. Everyone seems to have his or her own agenda, and each day seems to get crazier and crazier.

Talk about your last few days. Have family members each tell about what's been keeping them busy or what's been taking up their time. For a fun twist, spotlight one person at a time, and have the rest of the family tell what they think keeps that person busy.

Today's Memory Maker

Have each person grab an item that's "tossable." It'd be nice if the item represented something important to the person selecting it. Now stand in a circle. (You can define "circle" very loosely—especially if there are only two or three in your family.) Hand all the items to the family member whose birthday is closest to today. (Smile and say, "Happy birthday!")

Have that family member toss one item to someone in the circle, who will toss it to someone else, who will toss it to someone else, and so on until everyone has been tossed the item. Continue until you create a pattern of tossing and receiving. Always toss to the same person and receive from the same person.

Got that down? Now have that person slowly add the other items into the pattern of tossing and receiving. Continue until each person's item is in the juggling pattern.

Well, how'd you do? You can sit down now, and talk about what you just did. How did it feel to juggle everyone's stuff? Was it frustrating? fun? easy? difficult? How was juggling the items like trying to juggle your family's schedule of activities?

Today's Bible Insight

Pile all your items by the Bible, and look up Ephesians 5:15. Have the family member who's gotten the least amount of sleep this week read this verse. Hmm...what do you think it means?

- In what ways would God say we're living wisely? unwisely?
- How might God want us to make wiser use of our time?
- What could we do to make juggling our schedules easier?

Come up with a list of three specific ways that you can work together to live more wisely as a family. Then decide how you will put these ideas into action during the coming week. For instance, you may decide to set the alarm a half-hour earlier so you can have breakfast together. Or you might decide to drop one after-school activity so your family can spend more time together.

Our Family Prayers

Exchange items from the juggling activity. Then have family

members each pray for the person whose item they hold. Ask God for wisdom in using your time wisely.

If possible, keep the items to remind you to pray for each other during the week.

During the Week

Every time you see one of the juggled items...

• give a back rub or a hug to a stressed-out family member. If possible, help that family member with some of his or her responsibilities.

• remember God's words from Ephesians 5:15, but do it in a "juggling" kind of way. Pick up any tossable item, and toss it back and forth with a family member as you repeat the verse.

To help you juggle your schedules more effectively, make a list of all the scheduled, "must attend" events for the month (sports, clubs, church meetings, work, school, appointments) and the fun stuff you'd all like to do as a family. Number the list from most important to get done to least important. Then talk about how you will balance your responsibilities with your need to have fun together every week.

can love rub off?

TALK TOPIC: *Loving each other*

Our Family Stories

The words "I love you" mean a great deal, but love's actions mean even more. How do your family members know you love them? How can they tell how you feel?

Pause for a few moments, and reflect on love in your family. Allow each person to share how your family demonstrates love for one another. This can be a free-for-all with everybody getting a chance to say how love works. When do family members feel loved? not loved? Does anyone ever feel that he or she gives love but gets none in return? Do parents see more love or more fights between siblings? What do the kids see between parents? Talk about it.

Today's Memory Maker

Love requires more than words. It also demands action. To show how love rubs off on one another, give each family member a blank sheet of paper and a crayon or pencil. (Crayons without wrappers work best.) Then send each person away to find three items with different textures. Have them look for textures that are bumpy, squiggly, rough, smooth, or whatever. Then they can hold the paper against the objects and rub the crayons across the paper to make impressions of the surfaces' textures. (If younger family members need help with this, you can do this together rather than separately.)

When everyone has collected three rubbings, gather again and try to guess the source of each other's rubbings. If you'd like, select the funniest or the most interesting rubbing, and hang it up.

Then talk about your experience. How easy was it to identify the objects from their rubbings? How easy is it to tell how someone feels about you by the way he or she treats you? What kinds of actions leave others feeling loved? unloved?

Today's Bible Insight

Nowhere in the Bible is there a better description of love rubbing off on others than in 1 Corinthians 13. Some people have even dubbed it the "Love Chapter." The entire chapter is worth reading together, but if you're short on time, read 1 Corinthians 13:4-7 to discover how your love for your family can rub off on them.

Now take time to have each family member discuss at least two of the following ways love shows itself to others. For each statement you choose, discuss when and why it's sometimes hard to love like that.

• "Love is patient and kind."
• "Love is not jealous, it does not brag, and it is not proud."
• "Love is not rude, is not selfish, and does not get upset with others."
• "Love does not count up wrongs that have been done."
• "Love is not happy with evil but is happy with the truth."

• "Love patiently accepts all things. It always trusts, always hopes, and always remains strong."

If you're like most families, it's tough to love each other all the time. It's hard to be all those things that 1 Corinthians speaks about. But you can begin to "rub off" more love on each other.

Go back and have each person choose one of the characteristics of love that he or she wants to strive for during the coming week. Try to name one specific, measurable way to show that characteristic of love. Then have each person write or draw that personal "love goal" on one of his or her rubbings.

Our Family Prayers

Close with each person silently praying for God's help in rubbing off love to other family members. Have each person pray about the goal he or she mentioned earlier. Then place the rubbing pages on the refrigerator as reminders to love each other during the coming weeks.

During the Week

Every time you see your rubbings...

• show (and not just tell) someone in your family how much you love him or her.

• make other rubbings during the week to remind you to rub off more love to others.

Begin to memorize one or more of the verses from 1 Corinthians 13. How about the ending to verse 13: "And the greatest of these is love."

what are you afraid of?

TALK TOPIC: *Fear*

Our Family Stories

Every family has experienced fear. Maybe it was a new move. Or a scary illness. Or the loss of a job. Or the thought of divorce or death. Or just going to bed alone in the dark.

Tell each other about a time you were really scared. It can be recent or in the past. But it must be a fearful time. Be sure to talk about why you were scared and how you dealt with your fear.

Today's Memory Maker

People often equate fear with darkness. So although it may seem crazy, take the entire family to a dark place in your home. Check out a closet or some other small room that you can completely darken. If you're really inventive, you can make a blanket tent. The point is to be in the dark—together. One more thing, take a flashlight and your Bible with you.

Huddle together and talk about what it's like to be in the dark. Have each person share whatever he or she is feeling. Are you scared? Do you feel silly? How would you feel if you were all alone in the dark? Then think back to the fears you talked about earlier. How were they like being in the dark?

After you've discussed your fears, turn on the flashlight.

Today's Bible Insight

Shine the flashlight on your Bible, and look up John 12:46. Read aloud what Jesus said in this verse. Have everyone say those words together a few times. Then discuss the following questions:

- How is Jesus the light of the world?
- How does light help us not feel afraid?
- How does Jesus help us not feel afraid?

Then have each family member name one thing he or she is afraid of right now. It might be a bully at school, the prospect of losing a job, or simply being alone at night. After each person names a fear, brainstorm ways Jesus can help that person not be afraid.

Our Family Prayers

Have each family member hold the flashlight while he or she prays for faith to overcome the fear mentioned earlier. Close by having a volunteer thank God for sending Jesus as the light into our dark world.

During the Week

Every time you see a flashlight or headlights...

• remember that you don't need to be afraid because Jesus is the light of our world.

• find out from your family members how they keep from being scared about things happening in their lives.

To help you remember not to be afraid, repeat John 12:46 with a family member every time you turn on the lights or a lamp.

feeling upside down?

TALK TOPIC: *Disappointment*

Our Family Stories

Who hasn't hoped for something—and then had those hopes dashed? Maybe it was losing a game or missing the chance to play with someone we wanted to. Perhaps it was losing a good friend or not getting the promotion we'd been eyeing.

So take a moment to tell each other about the biggest disappointments you've ever experienced. Why were these things so disappointing? Then talk about a disappointment you've had recently. Give everyone a chance to share. And make sure you don't pass judgment on other people's heartbreaks. What may seem petty to one person may be a big deal to someone else. Listen with your hearts.

Today's Memory Maker

Now hand each person a spoon. Look into it as though it's a mirror. Then turn the spoon around and look at the other side. What happened to your reflection? (One way your reflection is right side up; the other way, it's upside down!) It doesn't matter how you hold the spoon when you start—your reflection will always look the opposite when you turn the spoon the other way! It's one of life's little surprises!

Take a moment to discuss your discovery. Why does the spoon reflect you right side up when you hold it one way and upside down when you hold it the other? How is this like what happens inside you when you experience a disappointment?

Today's Bible Insight

Now look up Matthew 5:4. Have a volunteer read Jesus' words while the rest of the family looks into their spoons. Repeat the verse together several times. Hold your spoon so your reflection is upside down when you start, then turn the spoon around when you say the word "happy." Then discuss the following questions:
- How does God comfort us when we're disappointed?
- How does this help turn our feelings "right side up"?
- How can we comfort someone who's feeling disappointed?

Brainstorm ways you can remind yourselves and each other of God's comfort whenever you experience disappointment. For example, you might talk about why the person is feeling disappointed, pray with the person and ask for God's comfort, perform the spoon experiment again, or something else.

Our Family Prayers

Now huddle together, and set your spoons in the center of your family. Wrap your arms around each other for a big hug. Then have each person pray for the family member on the left, asking God to give that person hope and encouragement.

During the Week

Every time you see or use a spoon...
- remember how Jesus can turn your disappointments upside down and turn them into something good.
- ask someone near you what he or she is most disappointed in. Then offer your help and support.

For extra fun, recite Matthew 5:4 whenever you use a spoon. Make sure you hold the spoon so your reflection is upside down when you start, then turn it around when you say the word "happy."

a personal connection

Our Family Stories

We all have questions about heaven. Even when we know that our loved ones who have died are in heaven—it's still hard to picture. So as a family, take a few minutes to talk about heaven. Talk about those already in heaven and why you can't wait to see them—maybe a grandparent, another relative, or a close friend. Make sure you recall some of your favorite memories with these people. Celebrate the fact that you'll see them again in heaven!

(This would also be a good time to talk about your concerns, struggles, or sadness if you have friends or relatives who didn't know Jesus when they died.)

Today's Memory Maker

Here's your family's opportunity to learn more about heaven. Find a four- to five-foot long piece of string, yarn, or jump-rope. Have everyone stand and hold onto the "rope." Walk together to a doorway, then have one person slip around the corner into another room, out of sight. Make sure that person doesn't let go of the rope.

While you're all holding the rope, have the family members in the first room answer the following questions:
• Where's (whoever is out of sight)?
• How do you know (name) is there?
• What does the rope do for us and (name)?

Then discuss how being connected to the person around the corner is like being connected to loved ones in heaven. How are they alike? How are they different? Who or what connects us to loved ones in heaven?

Today's Bible Insight

In John 14:1-3, 6, Jesus teaches us some important things about heaven. So take a few minutes to study these verses. Read each section of Jesus' words, then stop to answer the questions that follow.

Section 1: "Don't let your hearts be troubled. Trust in God, and trust in me" (John 14:1).

- Why would Jesus tell us not to be troubled?
- What do you think we are to trust Jesus for?

Section 2: "There are many rooms in my Father's house; I would not tell you this if it were not true. I am going there to prepare a place for you. After I go and prepare a place for you, I will come back and take you to be with me so that you may be where I am" (John 14:2-3).

- What do these verses teach us about heaven?
- What do you think is the best part about heaven?

Section 3: "I am the way, and the truth, and the life. The only way to the Father is through me" (John 14:6).

- Why is it important for everyone to believe in Jesus?
- How should we respond to God's gift of heaven to us?

Our Family Prayers

Tie the two ends of the rope together to create a circle. Have everyone hold onto the rope and thank Jesus for connecting them with God and with their loved ones in heaven.

During the Week

Every time you see a string or rope...

- think about the friends and family you'll see again when you go to heaven.
- work together to learn John 14:1. Then share what you learn with a friend.

For extra fun, create yarn pictures or posters filled with the words from John 14:1b: "Trust in God, and trust in me." (If you prefer, you can use John 3:16, a familiar favorite.) If you have friends who need to know more about Jesus, give them your yarn posters. Tell them you love them and want to see them in heaven.

pictures of love

Our Family Stories

No other bond of love is built into God's plan like the love among family members. But in a world messed up by sin, sometimes families hurt and struggle. Sometimes we need to stop and celebrate the connections we have as "family."

Take time to celebrate the love you've felt in your family. Let everyone talk about your family's bond of love. Do this by having family members each tell about a time they felt loved and what it was that made them feel that way. When everyone's done, have each one tell about a time he or she didn't feel loved and why.

Today's Memory Maker

Find a family photo album or a stack of pictures that bring back great family memories. Look through the pictures together and have each person decide which photo he or she thinks best represents your family's bond of love. Someone might select pictures from a favorite vacation or the church directory photo. Try to remember what each person was doing before and after the photo. Explain why the picture is special and how it represents your family's love.

Then give each person a sheet of paper and crayons or markers. Have everyone draw a picture that represents how your family treats each other every day. Encourage family members to be honest in their portrayals. It's OK if the pictures aren't as "loving" as you'd like.

When everyone is done, have family members each show and explain their pictures. Then discuss what the pictures reveal about your family. How do family members treat each other lovingly? How could you be more loving toward each other?

Today's Bible Insight

First John 3:11 packs a straight message about how we are to treat each other. Read the verse aloud, then discuss the following questions:

- How do you react when you're told that you "must" do something?
- Why does God want families to love each other no matter what?
- Why do you think it's so hard to love each other all the time?
- How could our family do a better job of obeying this command?

Give each person another sheet of paper. Have family members each draw a picture that depicts one way they'll act to show more love toward the other family members. When everyone's done, have each person describe what's happening in the picture. Then have each person commit to making that picture come true!

Our Family Prayers

Hold hands as a sign of your family's love for one another. Then have each person thank God for each family member's love and tell why that love is such a gift. Have the oldest family member conclude the prayer, thanking God for the best love of all—the love God had to send his Son, Jesus, to die for us.

During the Week

Every time you see a picture of a family member...

- give thanks to God for your family's love. Then show your love to the person (or people) in the picture.
- say, "I love you" to the nearest family member. Give that person a hug, too!

Whenever you're tempted to act unlovingly toward another family member, stop and recite 1 John 3:11 with that person.

---

oops! accidents happen!

TALK TOPIC: *Showing mercy*

Our Family Stories

Sometimes accidents happen—and it's nobody's fault. A cup of milk spills; a glass falls from the cupboard and breaks; a pie flies off the counter into a gloppy mess. Oops!

What happens in your family when accidents happen? Have everyone tell about a time he or she felt responsible for an accident. Tell all the details: how it happened, how other family members reacted, how you felt during and after the episode, and what happened when it was all over.

Today's Memory Maker

Get a plastic cup filled with water. Have a towel handy—just in case of spills! (Accidents happen, you know.) Sit in a circle. For the next minute, pass the cup of water around the circle as fast as you can. Try to not spill any water. Have fun with this game, and see how many times you can get the cup around the family without spilling.

After one minute, stop the game and talk about how each person felt during the game. Did everyone have fun? Was anyone nervous? If so, why? Was everyone working together? Or did someone try to get someone else to spill?

Now compare these feelings to what happens when someone in your family has an accident. How are those feelings similar? How are they different? How do your family members treat each other when someone gets in trouble?

Today's Bible Insight

We live in a world where accidents happen. God knew us, so he placed us together in families. Families can and should be a safe place for reaching out and supporting each other no matter what happens. Take out your Bible, and read Colossians 3:12. As one person reads the passage aloud, have the rest of the family pass the cup around again. But this time do it slowly as you all listen to God's Word.

To apply this verse to your family, discuss the following questions:

• Which of these words describe how you feel when you've had an accident?

• Which words describe how you treat other family members when they're responsible for an accident?

• What could your family members do to obey this command when accidents happen?

Have everyone name one way he or she will live out this teaching whenever an accident happens. For example, someone might say, "If Joey spills a glass of milk, I'll show mercy by helping clean it up."

Our Family Prayers

Join hands. Have everyone choose one of the words from Colossians 3:12—"mercy," "kind," "humble," "gentle," or "patient." Then have each person think of a specific way he or she can show that trait during the coming week. Close by having each person complete this sentence prayer: "God, help me be more _____ by _____ ."

During the Week

Every time you use a cup or glass…

• hand it to a family member and ask him or her to be "care-full" when you have accidents.

• remind each other that God showed mercy to you and wants you to show mercy to others.

For extra fun, fill glasses with different amounts of water to create a "water chime." Then "play" the glasses with a knife or a spoon as you recite Colossians 3:12 together.

are chores a bore?

Our Family Stories

Jobs are an inescapable part of living in a family. But life together goes so much better when everyone does his or her part. Usually that involves the dreaded "c" word: chores.

Have each family member tell about which chore he or she "adores." Then have each tell about which chore is the biggest "bore." (Parents may want to take the opportunity to bring up long lists of responsibilities they had when they were young!) Listen to everyone's story respectfully, but don't forget to have fun. A few moans and sighs and violin music in the background might add a nice touch! Have a good, playful time chortling about chores.

Today's Memory Maker

Line up behind a sink with soap and towels nearby. One by one, take turns washing each other's hands—gently and quietly. Then dry each other's hands—again gently and quietly. See if you can do all this without speaking. (If you're really brave, wash and dry each other's feet instead of hands!)

When you're finished, sit down and talk about your experience: Was washing each other's hands (or feet) easy or difficult? Explain. What did you like about this experience? What didn't you like? How are these feelings similar to how you feel about chores? How are they different?

Now get ready to hear a Bible story that's quite similar to what you just experienced.

Today's Bible Insight

Ask for a volunteer to read John 13:1-17—the story about Jesus washing the disciples' feet. Listen carefully to learn how Jesus' disciples reacted to Jesus washing their feet.

After the story has been read, have one person retell the story in his or her own words. Then discuss the following questions:

- How is this story like washing each other's hands? How is it different?
- What lesson was Jesus trying to teach his disciples by washing their feet?
- How can we apply Jesus' lesson by serving each other through our chores?

Now have each person tell how he or she can be a better servant at home. What chores can each person take on to serve the rest of the family? (You may want to write down these ideas for future reference.) Then have each person commit to doing one chore he or she named for the next week.

Our Family Prayers

Get the towel you used earlier. Have each person place a hand on the towel. Fill the towel with your family members' hands. Then close with each person praying to be a better servant by being a willing and cheerful "chore-doer."

During the Week

Every time you see or use a towel...

- serve a family member by doing one of his or her chores without being asked.
- thank Jesus for setting a perfect example of loving service for us to follow.

Once a day, take a towel to a family member and, while you both hold on to the towel, recite together Jesus' words in John 13:15: "I did this as an example so that you should do as I have done for you."

can i give you a hand?

Our Family Stories

One of the best things about love is giving it away. Families can bring extra joy by giving love away to people in need. I still remember going with my mom and grandma to visit lonely people in a nursing home.

What does your family do to help others? List all the ways that you help people who need a hand. What memories do you have about sharing God's love and blessings? Or maybe you have stories about others reaching out and helping you in times of need. Talk about that, too.

Today's Memory Maker

Sit in a circle. Place a canned good, boxed dessert, or sealed bag of candy in the middle of the circle. If at all possible, choose something that everyone in the family likes and that doesn't need further preparation. Then have each person talk about what he or she enjoys most about the food item you chose. Have fun as you try to outdo each other praising the taste and texture of your food item.

After several minutes, put the food item away and discuss how fun it was just to talk about the food item. What did you like about the experience? What didn't you like? How is this like talking about helping others but never doing anything about it? How is it different?

Then retrieve and enjoy your food item together. Take a few minutes to discuss how it feels when someone helps you out. Then tell how you feel when you help others.

Today's Bible Insight

Jesus loved to tell stories that had special meanings. One time Jesus told a story about the end of time. It's located in Matthew 25:31-46. Have one or more family members read the story while everyone else tries to identify the message Jesus wants to teach us today. (The passage is lengthy, so you may want to divide it up among several readers.)

After you've finished reading the story, take a few moments to talk about what Jesus was trying to teach. What does Jesus want us to do after hearing this story? Why does Jesus want us to help others?

Now think about how your family can put the story into practice today. Try to list specific ways your family can help those who are hungry, thirsty, lonely, in need of clothing, sick, and in prison. (It would be great if you wrote down several ideas for each one. That way you'd have a reminder to help others in various ways.)

Our Family Prayers

Together choose at least one helping action your family will commit to do. Decide when you'll do it. It's important that your entire family participate in helping others. Then pray that God will help your family to help others. Ask God to guide you as you keep your commitment. End with a family hug send-off!

During the Week

Every time you see your food item or a can of food...

• list all the ways Jesus teaches us to help others in Matthew 25:31-46.

• ask how you can help the person who's nearest you at the moment.

To remind you that it's important to serve others, every time another family member needs or asks for help, recite Matthew 25:40 together: "Then the King will answer, 'I tell you the truth, anything you did for even the least of my people here, you also did for me.'"

---

you're out of control!

Our Family Stories

One of the toughest things for us to do—no matter what our age—is to maintain our self-control. Two-year-olds throw temper tantrums when they're angry, but even older kids and adults slam doors, stomp around, and yell when they lose self-control.

So take some time right now to tell each other about a time you "lost it." Maybe it was the other day waiting in traffic when you blared the horn. Maybe it was when someone in the family didn't get ready in time, and you were late for a special appointment. As you tell your stories, take time to say you're sorry—especially if someone in the family was hurt by your loss of self-control.

Today's Memory Maker

For the next few minutes, play Honey, If You Love Me. It's a goofy game that will see how good you are at "self-control." Begin with the oldest family member as the "self-controlled one." Have the other family members attempt to get that person to smile. But here's the catch: Each person gets a turn to say, "Honey, if you love me, won't you please, please smile?" to the self-controlled one. No matter what the other family members do, the self-controlled one must reply to each person, "I love you, honey, but I just can't smile" without cracking a smile.

Give everyone a turn to try to make the self-controlled one smile, then switch roles and let others try to keep a straight face. Even though it sounds like a non-smiling game, it will produce lots of giggles.

When everyone's had a turn to be self-controlled, discuss how it felt trying not to smile. How difficult was it not to smile when others wanted you to smile? Talk about how this is like or unlike the times you lose your self-control in real life. If you didn't smile during the game, what kept you from smiling? How could you use ideas from your ability to be self-controlled in the game to being self-controlled in real-life situations?

Today's Bible Insight

The Bible tells us that God's Spirit working in us can help us overcome our selfishness, temper tantrums, and anger. We can't do it by ourselves. We need God's help. The good news is that God will help us. In Galatians 5:22-23, we learn about the fruit of the Spirit— what our lives look like when God is completely in control. Have someone read the passage aloud.

Just think! You'll never get in trouble when your life is filled with the fruit of God's Spirit. It's never wrong to be self-controlled! Take a moment to discuss the following questions:

- **How do you think God's Spirit produces self-control in us?**
- **What do we need to do to allow the Holy Spirit to do this?**
- **How can we help each other become more self-controlled?**

Now tell each other when it's hard for you to keep your self-control. Maybe one person throws a tantrum when no one wants to play a favorite game, while someone else starts yelling when the house is messy. Use this opportunity to ask forgiveness for times you've lost your self-control in the past and to ask for each other's help in becoming more self-controlled.

Our Family Prayers

Join hands together, and give each other big smiles. Then pray this two-part prayer. First, have each person complete this sentence: "Lord, forgive me for losing self-control when (name when you've lost your self-control)." Then have each person complete this sentence: "Lord, help me be more self-controlled when (name when it's hard to keep your self-control)."

During the Week

Every time you see a family member smile...

• gather one or more family members to play an impromptu round of Honey, If You Love Me.

• either ask God to forgive you for losing self-control or thank God for helping you keep your self-control.

To remind you that God's Spirit can help you overcome your hurtful impulses, practice listing together all the fruit of the Spirit, ending with a big "SELF-CONTROL!"

cleansing words

TALK TOPIC: *Forgiveness*

Our Family Stories

Every relationship that weathers time is built upon forgiveness. Great power lives in these three little words: "I forgive you." Unfortunately, some families are torn apart because family members can't find forgiveness for one another.

Tell each other stories about times you were forgiven. Make sure you mention who forgave you, why you needed to be forgiven, how it felt to be forgiven, and how being forgiven affected your relationship with the person who forgave you. Then talk about times forgiveness wasn't granted in your family. What happened to the people involved? Why didn't family members forgive each other? How do these stories make you feel?

Today's Memory Maker

Grab a page from a newspaper. Then have everyone name something for which he or she wants to be forgiven by another family member. Maybe it's for getting angry and yelling or for teasing someone until he or she cried. As family members name their wrongs, they must rub their hands on the piece of newspaper. Pass the newspaper from one family member to the next until everyone's had a chance to name something for which he or she would like to be forgiven.

Now talk about your experience. How does it feel to have your hands all dirty? What would it be like if you were never able to wash them? How is that like living with unforgiven sin?

Today's Bible Insight

Jesus is the ultimate forgiver. Can you believe it? He took all our sins on himself and willingly died on the cross so we could be forgiven and live with him forever.

Open your Bible to Colossians 3:13. (Be careful not to get newsprint on your Bible!) In this verse, Paul tells us what to do when someone does something hurtful. After reading the verse, take a moment to talk about it.

• Why are we supposed to forgive our family members?
• What will most likely happen if we don't forgive each other?

Then have family members forgive one another by using a wet, soapy cloth to wash off the newsprint ink. As each person gets "cleaned up," discuss how it feels to be forgiven. How is the cleansing of your hands like receiving forgiveness? Why is it important for family members to forgive each other? Who needs to make the first move when forgiveness is needed? What can we do to make sure we become a forgiving family?

Our Family Prayers

Join hands, clean hands! Then use this time to pray about forgiveness in your family. Start by taking turns asking each other for forgiveness for specific wrongs. (And remember—saying you're sorry means you're going to try not to do that wrong again.) Then have each person pray a silent prayer asking God for help forgiving others. Finally, close with one family member thanking God for his wonderful gift of forgiveness.

During the Week

Every time you see a newspaper...

•look at your hands, and say an eye-open prayer thanking God for his forgiveness of your sins.

•find the family member you seem to fight with most often, and recite Colossians 3:13 together.

To learn more about forgiveness, read the story of the prodigal son in Luke 15:11-32 or that of the unforgiving servant in Matthew 18:21-35. Talk about times you've seen similar events happen in your family.

them's fightin' words!

TALK TOPIC: *Communication*

Our Family Stories

Words hold great power. Kind words can cheer someone who's in a bad mood, while cruel words can change a smile into a frown in the flash of an eye. Because words hold such great power, God wants us to use our words with care.

Think back over the day (or yesterday). Then have family members take turns telling what words they heard that made them feel good. Who said the words and why? Then tell the opposite. What words did they hear that hurt? Why were these hurtful words said?

Today's Memory Maker

Give a sheet of typing paper or newspaper to someone in the family who likes crafts. Have that person fold the paper in half and cut out the shape of a paper doll person. (If scissors aren't handy, that person can be a ripper instead of a snipper! It's just important to have a paper doll person join your family for the next few minutes.)

Now pass the paper doll person around your family as you take turns saying words or phrases that hurt people and start fights. Maybe it's "Shut up!" or "Out of my room, stupid!" As family members say their hurtful words, have them rip off pieces of the paper doll person. Pass the paper doll person around the family at least twice. Bit by bit, the paper doll person will get ripped to pieces.

Talk about what it was like to rip apart your paper doll person as you said hurtful words. How did you feel when you said the hurtful words? when you ripped the paper doll person? How is this like ripping each other apart with hurtful words? How is it different?

Today's Bible Insight

Grab a Bible, and read aloud Matthew 5:9, one of the Beatitudes.

With this verse in mind, pass the torn paper doll person around your family again. Only this time, have each family member say a word or phrase that brings peace and stops fighting in your family. Maybe it's "I'm sorry. I was wrong to call you a name" or "I really want to listen to what you have to say."

Each time a "peacemaker" word or phrase is spoken, have the family member tape a piece of the paper doll person back where it belongs. Slowly, the paper doll person should begin to regain its shape. Continue until the paper doll person has been taped back together. (It's OK if the paper doll person isn't fixed perfectly. That helps make the point you're about to discover.)

Now have each person answer the following questions:

• How well were we able to put the paper doll person back together?

• How is this like trying to make up for hurtful words with kind ones?

• How can you use your words to create peace in your family this week?

Our Family Prayers

This will be a two-part prayer time. First, without joining hands, have each person offer a prayer of confession for times he or she used fighting or hurtful words.

After everyone has prayed, join hands. Ahhh...doesn't that feel better? Now have each person pray for the self-control and the wisdom to use his or her words to promote peace within the family.

During the Week

Every time you see a piece of tape...

• tear off a small piece of tape from a tape dispenser. Then say a kind word or phrase to a family member as you gently stick the tape to his or her finger as a reminder of your love.

• find a family member and talk about other ways your family can work together to be peacemakers.

For a fun way to remember God's Word, use the repaired paper doll person as a centerpiece to a poster that has the words to Matthew 5:9 written on it. Tape the poster to the refrigerator as a reminder that those who bring peace will be called God's children.

just trust me

TALK TOPIC: *Trusting each other*

Our Family Stories

Trust is like glue. When it's there, it can hold all the pieces of a family together. But if it's not, family life can fall apart pretty quickly!

Have family members each define or give an example of what "trust" means to them. Talk about times you trusted someone in the family and he or she didn't let you down. Talk about how it felt to trust that person. Then talk about the hard stuff. When did someone do something that made trust disappear? Everyone needs to talk about those times, too.

Today's Memory Maker

Pair up so that a large person and a small person are together. Have the large partner stand several feet behind the small partner. Instruct the small partner to shut eyes, fold arms, and stand really stiff—like a board. After the large partner promises to catch (never drop!) the small one, have the small partner fall over backward into the arms of the large partner. Do this until everyone gets a chance to be caught and to be the catcher. Have fun, but be careful!

When you're finished catching each other, sit together and talk about what you felt during the "trust fall." How did it feel to have to trust someone to catch you? to have others trust you to catch them? How are those feelings like everyday feelings of trust in your family? How are they different? What do you trust each other to do every day?

Today's Bible Insight

Working together as a family requires trust. Take a look at Ephesians 4:15-16 to learn what God's Word says about building trust. Then discuss the following questions:

• Why is "speaking the truth with love" important to building trust?

• How can breaking promises destroy trust among family members?

• What other kinds of actions might destroy trust within the family?

• What specific actions can we take to build trust within our family?

Our Family Prayers

Form a standing circle, and join hands. Hold tight! Now, can you lean back and hold each other up? Try it! You can hold each other up by trusting and supporting one another.

Lean forward and, while you're still holding hands, close with a special prayer for trust in your family. Have one person begin by praying, "Lord, I'm sorry I broke trust in my family by..." Have others also finish the same prayer sentence. Then conclude by having everyone forgive other family members for breaking trust and give thanks for the trust that exists.

Then have the entire family hold hands tightly, lean back, and say, "Amen!"

During the Week

Every time a family member holds his or her arms out...

• gather your family, and form a leaning circle like the one you formed during "Our Family Prayers."

• take turns catching and being caught by that person as a sign of your complete trust in each other.

To remind you to build family trust by speaking the truth in love, start each day by saying Ephesians 4:15 together. For extra fun, hold hands and lean back while you recite this verse.

---

i love you this much!

TALK TOPIC: God's love

Our Family Stories

Jesus loves us so much that he died for us. What a great sacrifice! He was willing to give up everything—even his life—because of his incredible love for us.

Families can show love through sacrifice too. Have each person think about a time a family member sacrificed or gave up something important to show love to him or her. Maybe Elizabeth didn't ask for a new bike because she knew Ethan needed clothes for school, or Dad went to the kids' concert instead of a football game. Talk about how you felt when someone sacrificed something for you.

Today's Memory Maker

Open a Bible to Romans 5:6-9. To get a better idea of Jesus' sacrifice for you, have each person stand with arms outstretched in the shape of a cross. Be sure family members keep their arms in this position until told to put them down. Everyone ready? Then arms out! Remember—no matter how much you want to drop your arms, keep them extended the way Jesus did on the cross.

After thirty seconds or so, talk about what you're feeling. How easy is it to keep your arms extended? What makes it hard for you to keep them up? How long do you think you could keep your arms up?

Today's Bible Insight

Now have one person read Romans 5:6-9. With arms still outstretched, think about what Jesus felt on the cross. Then discuss the following questions:

- How do you think Jesus felt while he was on the cross?
- Why do you think Jesus chose to suffer and die that way?

Everyone can put their arms down. Ahhh… (You might want to give each other shoulder and neck rubs to get your circulation going again.) Then take a few minutes to answer the following questions:

- How is our pain like what Jesus felt on the cross? How is it different?
- How do you think we should respond to Jesus' sacrificial love for us?
- How can we show Jesus' love to each other during the coming week?

Have each person tell at least one thing he or she will sacrifice during the coming week to show love to the rest of the family.

Our Family Prayers

Stretch out your arms like before, but this time put your arms around each other in a tight circle. Beginning with the tallest family member, have each person pray for help carrying out his or her promise of sacrificial love during the coming week—and beyond. Continue until everyone has prayed.

Then conclude your prayer by thanking God for the love he showed by sending Jesus to die on the cross. Have the shortest person say that prayer of thanksgiving for the entire family.

During the Week

Every time you see the shape of a cross…

• tell a friend about the love Jesus showed by dying to pay the penalty for our sins on the cross.

• think up a practical way to sacrifice your time or talents to show love to a family member.

To remind each other of Jesus' great sacrifice, stretch out your arms in the shape of a cross and say Romans 5:8 with a family member.

a direct connection

TALK TOPIC: *Prayer*

Our Family Stories

Prayer is simply talking to God—much like talking to anyone else that we love. It's especially great when families can talk to God together. Family prayers can be like getting together with special friends and relatives. God just loves getting together with us!

Take a few moments to tell about times you've talked with God. What did you say to God? Did you ask him for something special? Did you simply thank him for his love? How did God answer your prayer? Include favorite prayers from the past and special answers that God has given you recently.

Today's Memory Maker

Gather around your telephone. Then take a few moments to discuss how the telephone can help you understand prayer better. How is talking to someone on the telephone like talking to God in prayer? How is it different? How is praying like calling a good friend? What keeps you from calling good friends whenever you want? What keeps you from praying to God whenever you want? What does God want us to tell him when we pray? How does God want us to talk to him in prayer? If God were on the phone right now, what would you tell him?

After discussing the last question, have family members each pick up the phone and "talk" to God. Encourage everyone to tell God whatever is on his or her mind. One person might tell God about a problem at school, while someone else might ask God for a new friend. One last thing: Remember that God is listening, even when you're having fun.

Today's Bible Insight

The Bible talks about prayer in many places. James 5:13, for example, teaches that we can pray to God no matter what our situation. Read through the verse piece by piece, and then put what you learn into practice:

"Anyone who is having troubles should pray" (13a).
- What troubles does our family need God's help with?
- What can we ask God to do to help us with our troubles?

Now take a moment to ask God to help you endure or overcome your troubles. Remember to talk to God as though you were simply talking to a friend who knows you and loves you.

"Anyone who is happy should sing praises" (13b).
- What has God given to our family to make us happy?
- How can we praise God for the good he has done for us?

Now praise God for making your family happy. You might thank God for your home, tell him how wonderful he is for giving you one another, or simply tell God how much you love him.

Our Family Prayers

Surprise! You've already been having "family prayers"! And God *has* been listening! Close by thanking God for the gift of prayer and by praising God for the promise he made in James 5:16b: "When a believing person prays, great things happen."

During the Week

Every time you see a telephone...

• tell God about troubles you're having or praise God for the good things he's done for your family.

• find another family member, and recite the two halves of James 5:13 back and forth to each other.

For extra fun, begin a family prayer journal to record your prayers and how God answers them.

walk a mile in my shoes

TALK TOPIC: *Understanding each other*

Our Family Stories

Have you ever heard someone say, "I'd hate to be in his shoes" or "If you really want to understand her, you need to walk a mile in her shoes"? People use phrases like that because we associate "being in someone's shoes" with experiencing exactly what that person experiences.

So tell each other what it was like to be in your shoes today (or the day before). The point is to talk about what happened to you that you think others might have a hard time understanding. At our house, our son, Matt, might tell us about how hard it was to settle an argument with his best friend. And I might try to explain how exciting it was when we learned about the success of a new idea at work. Remember, it's impossible to give a "wrong" answer or put your foot in your mouth!

Today's Memory Maker

Here's a fun way to learn more about each other. Have each family member put one of his or her shoes in a pile. One by one, everyone must close his or her eyes and pull out a shoe. The only rule is that you can't grab your own shoe.

When everyone has a shoe, have family members *try* to put on the shoes. Then have everyone "become" the family member who belongs to the shoe. In other words, have family members take turns doing things that the shoes' owners normally do. For example, the person wearing the three-year-old's shoe might play with blocks, while the person wearing Mom's shoe might sort through the mail. Watch how easy or how difficult it is to "be" the other person.

Then sit in a circle, and talk about what it's like to be the owner of the shoe. Tell how you (the owner of the shoe) see yourself fitting into the family. Tell what you love about your family. Then tell what you wish people better understood about you—the stuff that you're not sure others really respect and appreciate.

When you've all had a chance to "walk a mile" in each other's shoes, discuss what it was like. What did you learn about each other? Any surprises? Was it easy or difficult to "be" the owner of the shoe? Why? How well do you really know and understand each other?

Today's Bible Insight

One way we show love and respect is by understanding what others feel and experience each day. God knew that secret. So he did something that only God can do. At the same time he was God, he became a human being to "walk a mile in our shoes." Read John 1:1-2, 14 to check this out.

Pick up the smallest shoe in the family, and use it as your "talk shoe." Whoever is holding the shoe gets to talk. Make sure to pass the shoe to each person so everyone gets a chance to answer each of these questions:

• Why do you think the God of the entire universe wanted to become a human being?

• How does knowing that Jesus has gone through what you're going through make you feel?

• What does this teach us about how we should treat people we don't understand?

One by one, draw a shoe out of the pile and tell how each of you can treat the owner of the shoe with more love and respect during the next week. In other words, tell how you will be more like Jesus to one another.

Our Family Prayers

Exchange shoes one more time. Now pray for the owner of the shoe that you're each holding. Offer words of thanks to God and encouragement for that person.

During the Week

Every time you put on your shoes...

• switch roles and "become" the family member nearest you for the next five minutes.

• imagine Jesus putting on your shoes. What would he think, do, and say in those shoes?

Play a game to remember the first half of John 1:14. Tap someone else's shoe, and then race to say, "The Word became a human and lived among us." See who can say the verse first!

to tell the truth

TALK TOPIC: *Honesty*

Our Family Stories

Being truthful with each other strengthens families because it builds trust between family members. But when people (including family members) aren't honest with each other, that dishonesty breaks down trust.

It's time to tell the truth—on yourselves. Tell stories about a time you weren't totally honest with someone. Maybe it was during a project at work. Maybe it was a time you weren't really where you said you'd be or you didn't really do what you had promised, such as brush your teeth or do your chores. Whatever it was, tell about that incident. What happened? How did you feel when you knew you weren't being truthful? What did your dishonesty do to your relationship with the person to whom you were dishonest?

Today's Memory Maker

Here's a test of truth that will help everyone see how important being honest really is. Have family members each think of four things to tell about themselves. The only catch is that one of those things must be a fib. While people are coming up with their "fib lists," have one person find something around the house to be a "crown of truth" to place on the speaker's head. For example, you might use a baseball cap or paper cut into the shape of a crown. See what you can find.

When everyone has a list, place the crown of truth on the person's head who's telling about himself or herself. Then see if the rest of the family can figure out which one of the four statements is a fib. Pass the crown from person to person until everyone's had a chance to tell his or her fib.

When you've finished your test of truth, talk about it. This time you must tell the truth about what you're thinking and feeling. How easy was it to think up a fib? to tell the fib? What were you feeling when you were fibbing? How did you feel when others were fibbing to you? How is this like telling lies in real life? How is it different? Why is it difficult to tell the truth all the time? Why is lying so hurtful?

Today's Bible Insight

God knows the value of truthfulness, and so do kings. Take a look at Proverbs 16:13. Keeping in mind the importance of speaking the truth, take several moments to discuss the following questions:
- Why do you think kings like honest people?
- Why do *you* like people who tell the truth?
- Why should you tell the truth all the time?
- How does honesty help strengthen our family?

Then take turns telling each other when it's hard to tell the truth and why. After everyone has shared, brainstorm ways you can help each other tell the truth even when it's hard. For example, family members could promise to *honestly* praise a family member who has a habit of lying to make himself or herself look better.

Our Family Prayers

Have the person who did the best job of guessing the fibs hold the crown of truth and pray about his or her struggle to be honest. The prayer can be a confession for lying or a request for God's help in telling the truth. Pass the crown around the family until each person has had a chance to pray about his or her struggle to tell the truth. Then set the crown of truth in a visible place so everyone will remember the value of truth-telling.

During the Week

Every time you see your crown of truth...
- ask yourself if you've lied to someone recently. If so, confess your lie to that person.
- pray for God's strength to tell your family members the truth even when it's hard.

Every time you hear the words "truth" or "lie," find a family member and recite to each other Proverbs 16:13.

sweet success

TALK TOPIC: *Problems*

Our Family Stories

We all experience times of success...as well as times we feel like total failures. Failure can be pretty hard to take, but family members can make it easier by understanding and supporting each other during the roller coaster of life's ups and downs.

To discover how well you know each other, try to answer the questions below for each other. Read the first question, then have everyone think about how the oldest family member might answer that question. Don't let anyone answer until everyone's thought of an answer. Then, when everyone else has shared his or her answer, the oldest family member can tell how accurate (or inaccurate) the answers were. Repeat the process for the second oldest family member and so on until everyone has guessed about everyone else. Repeat the same process with the second question, but start with the youngest family member this time.

- When have you felt most successful?
- When have you felt most like a failure?

Today's Memory Maker

Set out a pitcher of milk, unsweetened cocoa, a stirring spoon, and a glass for each family member. Announce that you're going to make chocolate milk. (If it's cold outside, you may want to heat up the milk first and prepare hot chocolate.) Slowly add cocoa to the milk until the color of your chocolate milk is just right. It may take awhile for the cocoa to dissolve in the milk, so keep stirring.

Then serve everyone chocolate milk and begin talking about how well you were able to answer the questions in "Our Family Stories" for each other. Were there any surprises? If so, what were they?

Before long, family members will probably complain that the chocolate milk tastes bitter. When that happens, use this teachable moment to compare the "failed" chocolate milk to the failures you discussed earlier. What's your opinion of the chocolate milk? What do you think is wrong with it? How can we make the chocolate milk taste better?

Add sugar to the glasses of chocolate milk to sweeten it to taste. Then talk about how drinking bitter chocolate milk is like experiencing failure in real life. How are they similar? How are they different? What can you do to make failure easier to swallow?

Today's Bible Insight

Everyone experiences failure, but Jesus can turn the bitterest failures into the sweetest successes. Take a look at John 16:33 to discover how. Then, while you're enjoying your chocolate milk, discuss the following questions:

- How does it feel to know you'll have troubles in this world?
- How can Jesus' words help us be brave when we fail?

• How can Jesus help us overcome our failures? feeling like failures?

Then brainstorm ways Jesus turned (or could turn) the bitter failures you talked about earlier into sweet successes. For example, maybe someone who failed a test learned the importance of studying. Finally, have each person list one way other family members can help him or her remember in the future that Jesus turns our bitter failures into sweet successes.

Our Family Prayers

Add sugar until the chocolate milk in the pitcher is sweet. Then serve each other chocolate milk, making sure everyone has a full glass. Hold your glasses up in thanks to God. Then have one person pray, thanking God for the peace we have in Jesus and asking God to help family members bravely trust him even when they experience failure.

Then enjoy your chocolate milk together while you discuss other good things God brings out of our failures.

During the Week

Each time you see a glass or a container of milk...

• find a nearby family member, and promise that you'll be there to help him or her through any troubles.

• thank God for helping you overcome failure, and ask him to help you trust him through every failure.

Work together with your family to learn John 16:33. Maybe you could turn this into a game, having each family member recite the verse whenever he or she takes a drink of milk.

doing unto others...

TALK TOPIC: *Golden Rule*

Our Family Stories

It's really special when someone cares about us enough to treat us the way we want to be treated. So celebrate what each family member does that you really like.

Tell each other about a time another family member treated you in a way you're thankful for. Explain why it made you feel so good. For example, Mom might tell about the morning that the kids brushed their teeth, made their beds, and got dressed without being asked. Use this opportunity to give each other a pat on the back for the nice things you do for one another.

Today's Memory Maker

Set out snack plates, a set of measuring cups, and a favorite family snack that you have on hand, such as M&M's, trail mix, peanuts, dried fruit, or cereal. Ask family members to fix snack plates for each other (making sure no one gets left out!) by measuring out the amount of snack they think that family member deserves. One more thing—you can't talk while you're fixing each other's snacks!

When the snacks are ready, announce that family members must keep the plates they fixed. The snack they prepared is the snack they are to eat.

Then, while you're all enjoying your snacks, discuss your reaction to the experience. How do you feel about getting the snack that you prepared? Would you have chosen the same amount if you'd known you were fixing your own snack? Why or why not? What does this reveal about how we as family members treat each other?

Today's Bible Insight

In Matthew 7:12a, Jesus teaches us to treat each other according to the Golden Rule. A rule is a way of measuring if something is correct, so we can know how to treat our family members by measuring our actions against the Golden Rule.

Open your Bible to Matthew 7:12a. Read Jesus' Golden Rule aloud, and discuss the following questions:

• How would this rule apply to our fixing each other's snacks?
• In what ways do we do a good job of following the Golden Rule?
• When have we failed to follow this guideline as well as we could?
• What can we do every day to put the Golden Rule into practice?
• If each of us acted this way, how would our family be different?

Our Family Prayers

Form a circle. Place the snack, the measuring cups, and the plates in the center of your circle. Then have everyone fix a snack for the family member on his or her right. To help you remember to follow the Golden Rule, have everyone serve the other family member whatever amount of snack that family member asks for.

Then, before everyone enjoys this snack, have family members take turns praying, asking God to forgive them for times they didn't follow Jesus' Golden Rule and committing themselves to treat each other as they want to be treated during the coming weeks.

After a family "amen," enjoy the snacks that you've prepared for each other.

During the Week

Each time you see or eat the favorite snack...

• ask a family member what he or she would like you to do, and then do exactly what that person asks.

• pray a silent prayer asking God to help you follow Jesus' Golden Rule with your family members.

Every time your family enjoys a snack together, work together to learn and recite Matthew 7:12a.

a time to laugh

TALK TOPIC: *Laughter*

Our Family Stories

A family that laughs together generally loves a lot! They don't laugh at someone's misfortune or make fun of, hurt, or tease each other. They simply laugh for fun.

Take some time to tell each other the last time you remember getting the giggles or belly laughs with someone in your family. As you recall those times, explain why it brings you chuckles all over again.

Today's Memory Maker

When was the last time your family played a game together? Well, here's a new one. It's called Thumper. There's nothing serious about this game. It's a game of silly sight and sound that each family member helps to invent. Ready?

Have everyone dream up a funny action and a sound. For example, someone might put a thumb in each ear, wave both hands, and say, "Whee!" Allow a few minutes for family members to think up and demonstrate trademark signs and sounds for Thumper.

When everyone has a sign, have the oldest family member begin the game as follows: Start slapping both hands on your knees for a thumping sound, then ask everyone else to join in. Ask, "What's the name of this game?" Everyone should reply, "Thumper!" Then ask, "How do we play?" They should say, "Thump!"

While the rest of the family is thumping, make your sign and sound and then someone else's sign and sound. Then the person whose sign and sound you gave must give his or her sign and sound and then someone else's sign and sound. Continue doing this until someone messes up either his or her sign and sound or someone else's sign and sound.

After a blooper, have the next oldest person start the game over again. However, this time the person who made the mistake can only thump, and no one can give that person's sign anymore—or that'll be a mistake! All this just confuses the rest of the family!

Play until you want to stop. Or play until each person has had a chance to start the game. Thumper is really silly and just for fun, so laugh it up!

Today's Bible Insight

Often we think the Bible is just a book of serious, solemn stuff. And some people think Christians can't have any fun. Well, that's not true. Take a peek at Ecclesiastes 3:1 and 4, then discuss the following questions:

- Why do you think God created a time for us to laugh?
- When is it a good thing to laugh? When is it not good?

Keep what you just learned in mind as you see how your family rates in the laughter department. Have one person read the list while the rest of the family answers each question. Use a thumbs up for yes, and a thumbs down for no.

- Do we laugh together quite a bit?
- Do we seem mad or sad a lot?
- Do we enjoy each other's company?
- Do we fight with each other a lot?
- Do we laugh when someone gets hurt?
- Do we enjoy fun activities together?

Now talk about what you learned about your family. What surprised you about your answers? Is there anything you would like to change? If so, what? What will you do this week to help your family become a loving and laughing family?

Our Family Prayers

For fun, draw a tiny smiley face on the tip of each person's pointer finger with a pen or skinny watercolor marker. Then use the smiling finger to point to the person you're giving thanks for. Have each family member point to each person and say, "Thank you, God, for (name). You make me laugh when..."

During the Week

Every time you hear someone laughing...

- give that person a thumbs up sign, touch pointer fingers, and recite Ecclesiastes 3:4 together.
- start a family "laugh-it-up" chart that keeps track of funny things that happen during the week.

To learn more about laughter, read Genesis 18:1-15; 21:1-7 to learn what the name "Isaac" means. You'll find a story that demonstrates how God loves to make his people laugh.

love lights

Our Family Stories

Chances are, you can probably think of people you don't like to be around. Maybe you don't like the way they look or act or talk. Something about them just irritates you. What *really* bugs you?

Take a few minutes to get those "bugs" off your chest. For example, you might be bothered by people who eat with their elbows on the table, by kids who won't share, or by "interruptions." Get those bugs out by finishing this sentence: "What *really* bugs me is..." (It's OK if you have more than one thing to tell about.)

Today's Memory Maker

Now find and light a candle. (Even an old birthday candle will work.) Explain that the candle is like love, that we want to keep it going all the time. Then have the family stand in a straight line, and give each person the chance to carry the lighted candle past the family while they try to blow it out. (Adult family members, use your best judgment about young family members carrying the candle. Little ones can make great blower-outers!) The only rules are that the person carrying the candle can't shield the candle or walk farther than three feet away from the family line. See who can carry the candle past the family line without getting it blown out.

After everyone who can has carried the candle, sit in a circle, and talk about your experience. What made it hard to carry the candle without getting it blown out? What makes it hard to love people who bug us? How are things that bug us like a wind that blows out our love for others? What could we have done to keep the candle lit? What can we do to love people who bug us?

Today's Bible Insight

Locate Matthew 5:43-48 in your Bible. Ask a volunteer to read these verses while everyone else tries to discover how we are to treat people who bug us and why.

Now spend several minutes discussing the following questions:

• How does God want us to treat people who bug us?

• Why should we treat people who bug us this way?

Matthew 5:14-16 gives us another reason we should love people who irritate us. Jesus said, "You are the light that gives light to the world. A city that is built on a hill cannot be hidden. And people don't hide a light under a bowl. They put it on a lampstand so the light shines for all the people in the house. In the same way, you should be a light for other people. Live so that they will see the good things you do and will praise your Father in heaven."

• How can we show the light of God's love to people who bug us?

• What will you do this week to show love to someone who bugs you?

Our Family Prayers

Read Matthew 5:44 again. It says that we're to pray for those who hurt us. The same holds true for those who irritate us. So join hands together, and have family members each pray for one person who bugs them. Be sure that each person asks God to help him or her show the light of his love to that person during the coming week.

During the Week

Every time you see a candle...

• think about how you've been treating someone who bugs you—then pray for that person.

• try to remember all the reasons God wants us to love people who bug us or even try to hurt us.

To help your family remember to shine God's love to everyone, turn out the lights every night, light a candle, and say Matthew 5:44 together.

---

oh, baby!

Our Family Stories

Families' greatest beginnings happen around babies! Everyone thinks it's a big deal when a baby arrives! Even God thinks so!

Have family members each tell something they know about when they were born. Parents might add some favorite stories by completing the sentence: "What I remember most about you as a baby is..." Do this for each member of the family. Then let children ask about what Mom or Dad were like as babies. (If children are adopted or joined the family after "babyhood," use this as a time to celebrate what you do know about their special birth.) It would also be fun to call or write grandparents for added details. They know a lot!

Today's Memory Maker

This is the time to unearth those family albums. Or maybe you have pictures around the house of family members when they were babies. Round them up, and take several moments to ooh and aah over the baby pictures. Use this time to recall favorite stories about each person when he or she was tiny.

Have everyone pick his or her favorite baby picture. Family members can select pictures of themselves or of other family members, but they need to explain why they picked those pictures. Then talk about how each member of the family is important to the family. What makes each person unique in our family? What's the best thing that person brings to our family? Complete this sentence for each family member: "Our family wouldn't be complete without (name) because..."

Today's Bible Insight

You've been a gift to your family during your lifetime—and a gift to God for a long, long time. According to the Bible, God had big plans for each person before he or she was ever born! Pull out your Bible, and have someone read the poem in Psalm 139:13-16. Then take a few moments to discuss these questions:

- Why do you think each one of us is so precious to God?
- How does God show us how important we are to him?
- When do your family members make you feel important?
- How can you make other family members feel important?

To apply what you've learned, have each family member choose one way to make every other family member feel important or valued during the coming week. For example, Dad might have lunch with each child and take Mom out on a special date, while one of the kids might choose to write thank you notes for each person in the family.

Our Family Prayers

To close, read the prayer on page 74 for each person. (If you'd like, you can make a photocopy for each family member, and write his or her name in the blanks.) Pray it completely for each person as the other family members put their hands (as a sign of blessing) on the person's head you're praying for.

During the Week

Every time you see a baby or a picture of a baby...

- give thanks for that baby's life, and then recite Psalm 139:14 as a prayer of thanks to God.
- get with a nearby family member, and talk about more of your favorite baby memories.

For extra fun, use the "Psalm 139:13-16" handout as a special page to illustrate as an addition to your family's photo album or scrapbook. Work together to create a special work of art that will add to your family memories.

Psalm 139:13-16

You made _____ 's whole being;

you formed _____ in (his/her) mother's body.

I praise you because you made _____ in an amazing and wonderful way.

What you have done is wonderful. I know this very well.

You saw _____'s bones being formed

as _____ took shape in (his/her) mother's body.

When _____ was put together there,

you saw _____'s body as it was formed.

All the days planned for _____ were written in

your book before _____ was one day old.

We thank you, heavenly Father, for_____. Amen.

we're one in Christ

TALK TOPIC: *Loneliness*

Our Family Stories

It's awful to feel alone. Apart. Isolated. Disconnected. Loneliness can happen when you're by yourself—but it can also happen when you're around other people. That's what's so weird about feeling alone. Sometimes you can feel it without anyone else noticing.

Have family members each tell about a time this week they felt apart or isolated from the family or from one particular family member. As you each tell your story, tear a sheet of toilet tissue into tiny squares to represent your feelings of "apartness." Place all the tiny squares in one heap. (Remember to listen with your heart as others talk about their loneliness. This is no time for making jokes.)

Today's Memory Maker

When we're feeling all alone, there is one person who can bring us all together. That person is Jesus Christ—the great connector. When problems or unfortunate circumstances separate families, they can still be connected in Jesus.

To demonstrate how Jesus brings families together, ask a volunteer to take a comb and comb through his or her hair a few times. (This should create some nifty static electricity!) Now hold the comb over the tissue pieces. Watch what happens! The comb draws all the pieces together! Ta-da!

Give everyone a chance to do the experiment. Then take a few minutes to talk about things that make you feel alone. When do you feel most lonely? least lonely? How would it feel if our family were separated? What problems or situations might separate us as a family?

Today's Bible Insight

Now take a look at what Ephesians 2:12-14, 19b teaches. To help you understand and apply these verses to your family, discuss these questions:

• How is Jesus' love like the "electrified" comb? How is it different?

• How are we like the pieces of toilet tissue? How are we different?

• What should it mean to us that we are members of God's family?

• What should we remember when our family becomes separated?

• What can we do to build the family unity God wants us to have?

Our Family Prayers

Have someone "electrify" the comb once again, and watch the pieces come together as you pray an eye-open prayer. Have one family member pray for God's help to keep (or bring) your family together. Include a prayer for each person's time mentioned earlier when he or she felt apart from the family. Pray that Jesus' love can be shown as you all work together to be a family of love in Christ.

During the Week

You guessed it—every time you see a roll of toilet tissue...

- put a few squares of paper in your pocket or purse as a reminder that you're never all alone.
- remember to tell your family members whenever you feel isolated, alone, or apart from them.

For extra fun, grab a roll of toilet tissue, and keep it in a prominent place during the week. Then, whenever you think of it, write on the roll the words from Ephesians 2:19b: "You belong to God's family!" See how long a banner you can create! It'll help you remember the Bible verse in a fun sort of way!

TALK TOPIC: *Accepting each other*

Our Family Stories

It's important for families to be friends. Sometimes we forget that and think friends are people who aren't in the family. But God wants us to be just as nice to our family members as we are to our closest friends.

To see what this might look like, tell each other about a person who's been a special friend to you. (This time tell about friends outside the family. Save family friendships for later.) What makes this person a special friend? What do you like to do with this friend? What do you like most about this friend? How does this friend make you feel?

Today's Memory Maker

Find a blanket. It can be an afghan, a baby blanket, or any other kind of blanket. For the next few moments, pass the blanket around the family, and have each family member "act out" with the blanket however he or she feels about your family. No words allowed! For example, Ginny might snuggle with the blanket to show that she feels close and happy in her family. Or Billy might put the blanket on a chair far away to show that he feels he doesn't fit in anymore.

Watch and listen with your hearts. When everyone's finished, guess what each "blanket action" was meant to convey. Then have family members each explain why they did what they did with the blanket. Talk about what this reveals about how friendly your family is. In what ways is your family friendly? unfriendly? Whom do you treat better—friends or family members? Explain. How could your family treat each other more like friends?

Today's Bible Insight

God wants us to be friendly to all people, especially our families. Read Romans 15:5-7 to discover what this involves. Then discuss these questions to apply this Scripture to your family:
- What makes it hard for family members to accept each other?
- What could we do to become more accepting of one another?
- How will accepting one another make our family friendlier?

Take turns saying one thing each person can do to be more accepting of other family members during the coming week. For example, someone might promise not to criticize the way another looks or dresses. Someone else might commit to paying attention when another talks.

Our Family Prayers

Have everyone grab hold of the blanket. Have each person pray silently about some area in which he or she finds it difficult to accept another family member. After a minute or so, take turns praying aloud, asking God to help you keep your commitments to be more accepting of each other.

During the Week

Every time you see a blanket...

• use it to "hug" another family member while you tell that person that you accept him or her.

• think of something you can do to be a friendly family member, then do it—secretly, if you can!

Every night when you tuck someone in or get tucked in, say Romans 15:7 with that person.

such sweet words!

TALK TOPIC: *Thankfulness*

Our Family Stories

"Hey, thanks!" It feels so good to hear those words once in a while. That's why parents try so hard to teach little kids to say "please" and "thank you" to others. But sometimes we're much better at thanking people outside our family than we are at telling family members when we're thankful. So here's a chance to give thanks in your family.

First, get in touch with how it feels to be thanked. Let family members each tell about a time someone made them feel good by thanking them. Then have everyone tell something a family member did that he or she appreciated but never said "thank you" for. Use this time to express your thanks for what that person did.

Today's Memory Maker

In many ways, giving and receiving thanks is a lot like eating dessert! So find something sweet to eat—perhaps a small piece of candy or a piece of fruit. (Try to find something that everyone likes.) Have everyone take a tiny bite and savor the taste. Tell what you like most about this treat.

Then talk about sweet things you like. What is your all-time favorite sweet? Why do you like that sweet so much? When do you crave that sweet? What would you do if you couldn't have that sweet? What would life be like if there were no sweets at all?

Today's Bible Insight

Did you ever wonder why parents (and God) want us to say thanks to each other? Open your Bible to Proverbs 16:24 for a clue.

Yum! Now take a few minutes to discuss the following questions:
- How are words of thanks like a yummy sweet treat?
- How often do we express our thanks to each other?
- What would happen if we thanked each other more?
- In what ways can we express our thanks to each other?

Then help each other brainstorm ways to say or express thanks to other family members during the week.

Our Family Prayers

Starting with the youngest family member and working your way to the oldest, have a "thankfest" prayer for each person. Join hands in a circle, and have everyone complete the following sentence for each person: "I'm thankful for (name) because..."

Then conclude your prayer with a "sweet" hug. Take turns becoming the center of a family "cinnamon roll." The center person simply needs to let go of one hand while the rest of the family spirals around him or her (with hands still held). After someone's gotten wrapped around like a cinnamon roll, give that person a giant squeeze!

During the Week

Every time you see a sweet, scrumptious treat...
- think of one person to say thanks to with a note, a phone call, kind words, or a treat.
- pray for your family, then fix a special snack or drink to show your thanks to them.

To remind you to "feed" each other with your words, recite Proverbs 16:24 together before every meal.

the ties that bind

Our Family Stories

Families are bound together by all kinds of promises—the promise to love, the promise to accept, the promise to support. Unfortunately, families are often torn apart when promises are broken.

Have family members each tell about a time they made a promise—and then broke it. What happened? Why did you break your promise? How did you feel after you broke the promise? How did it affect your relationship with the other person?

After everyone's told a story, tell about times the opposite happened—when someone made a promise to him or her and kept it! How did that feel? How did it affect your relationship with the other person?

Today's Memory Maker

When someone says, "I promise," he or she means "I won't break my word. I'll do what I said I'd do." Sometimes people use rings to symbolize that they've made a promise. So make a human ring by holding hands in a circle. Hold tight and lean back. Wow! You made a circle that supports itself! Now list all the reasons you can think of that people keep the promises they make.

Lean forward but continue holding hands. Then take turns telling why someone would break a promise. But here's the catch. Whoever is speaking must try to break away from the hand-holding circle. Watch what happens to the strength of your hand-holding circle.

When everyone's tried to break away, sit down and talk about what you learned. How did it feel when you held each other together?

when you started breaking apart? How is this promise circle like what happens in real life when promises are kept? are broken?

Today's Bible Insight

God's promises to us are like perfect rings that can't be broken. Have a volunteer read God's promise in Romans 8:37. Then discuss the following questions to discover what this means to your family:

• When do you feel that God might not keep his promises? Why?

• How can our family follow God's example of promise-keeping?

• What should we do when we break a promise to someone else?

• What should we do when someone else breaks a promise to us?

• What promises should our family members make to each other?

Our Family Prayers

Have a family celebration of promises kept—especially God's promise to love you and your promise to love each other. Have one family member donate a ring from his or her finger to use during the prayer time.

Have the person holding the ring say to each family member, "(Name), God promises to love you forever—and so will I!" For fun, place the ring on each other's fingers while you repeat this. Make sure each person says this to each family member. Then have one person close in prayer, thanking God for the promise of his love and asking God to help you be a promise-keeping family.

During the Week

Every time you see a ring shape (a wedding ring, Cheerios, Life Savers, an inner tube—you get the picture)...

• turn to a family member and say, "Look, I found a symbol of God's promise of love!"

• hold hands to make a ring with other family members as you recite Romans 8:37 together.

As a reminder of the importance of keeping your promises, give each other inexpensive rings (even plastic ones will do) to wear all week.

in God we trust

TALK TOPIC: *Trusting God*

Our Family Stories

Who can you trust these days? It seems as though a lot of people are afraid to trust anyone. We don't know who we can rely on, and even the people we trust sometimes let us down.

Take a few minutes to tell each other about someone or something you trust. What about the trustworthy person makes him or her reliable to you? Is it a neighbor who always tells the truth or someone who always remembers to send a birthday card? What is it about that person that causes you to trust him or her? Or what causes you to trust a certain thing? Does your car always start—even when it's cold?

Narrow down the traits of people and things that *can* be trusted. Write them down, if you'd like.

Today's Memory Maker

Now grab a U.S. penny, and get ready to make some "cents" out of your trust talk. Examine the penny together. Find the phrase that talks about trust, and read it out loud together. Why do you think the penny has this phrase on it?

Now play a quick game of Heads or Tails with the penny. Have the youngest family member be the "penny tosser" and give the penny a nice flip into the air just before everyone else calls out whether it will land on heads or tails. Have guessers keep track of how many times they guess correctly. Play at least five rounds, but no more than ten—so you don't run out of fingers to keep score!

Then talk about how playing Heads or Tails is like guessing who you can and can't trust. How accurately did you guess how the penny would land? What does this reveal about how well you can trust your guesses? How well can you guess who can be trusted? who can't be trusted? What happens when we trust people who can't be trusted? when we don't trust people who can be trusted?

Today's Bible Insight

Have the family member who most resembles Abraham Lincoln on the penny read Proverbs 3:5. Then pass the penny from person to person as you take turns answering the following questions (only the person holding the penny may talk!):

- What is it about God that makes him totally trustworthy?
- Why can't we trust our own understanding all the time?
- What might happen if we trust ourselves instead of God?
- When is it hard for you to trust God with all your heart?

Then have each person name one thing for which he or she needs to trust God right now. If possible, help each other think of ways you can build more trust in God in those areas.

Our Family Prayers

Have one person hold the penny so you can see the phrase "in God we trust." Then have that person thank God for being totally trustworthy and ask God for help trusting him for the situation mentioned earlier. Pass the penny around until everyone has had a chance to hold the penny and pray.

During the Week

Every time you see a penny...

• play Heads or Tails with a twist. Each time the penny comes up heads, tell about a time you trusted God. When it lands on tails, tell about a time you forgot to trust God and depended on your own understanding.

• be the first person in your family to start saying Proverbs 3:5. The rest of the family can join in, so by the end of the week you'll all know the verse by heart.

For fun, collect all the pennies you've got stashed around the house. Then together donate the money to a special cause. It could be a local food bank or a missionary your church sponsors. That way God will be working through you so others can see the power of trusting in God!

it's ok to cry

TALK TOPIC: *Crying*

Our Family Stories

When there's a baby in the house, everyone expects to hear crying. Crying is the only way a tiny baby knows how to say that it's hungry, that it needs a diaper change, or that it's tired. As we get older and catch on to this communication thing, we really don't need to cry as much. But sometimes we go to the opposite extreme and think it's bad or wrong to cry.

Since tears represent feelings, tell about the last time you cried—
or felt like crying but didn't. Explain why you cried, and what was
going on inside of you that made you feel like crying. Listen to each
other sympathetically, really trying to understand each other's feelings.

Today's Memory Maker

Now bring out a box of tissues. One by one, have each family
member pull out a tissue and tell when it's OK to cry. For example,
someone might say when someone you love dies, when you get hurt,
when you see a sad movie, or even when you're incredibly happy.
Keep pulling out tissues until you can't think of any more times it's
OK to cry.

When you can't think of any more OK "crying times," talk about
what you learned. What surprises you about the number of tissues
you pulled out? Are there a lot? not very many? What does this tell
you about when it's OK to cry? Are there times it's not OK to cry?
When might it be wrong to cry? Is crying allowed in your family very
often? Why or why not?

Today's Bible Insight

Jesus showed us how to live, but there's one thing Jesus did that
we don't talk about very often—a time Jesus cried. Have a family
member turn to John 11:1-44, a famous story about Jesus and his
friends Mary, Martha, and Lazarus. The story is pretty long, so while
it's being read, have the listeners close their eyes and picture the story
unfolding before them!

When you're done reading the story, have family members open
their eyes and talk about all the feelings they imagined going on in
that story. (You could even use the tissues you pulled out earlier to
represent those feelings.) Then read John 11:35 again, and discuss the
following questions:
- When have you felt as sad as the people in the story?
- Why do you think Jesus cried before he raised Lazarus?
- What things in the world might make Jesus cry today?
- How can we follow Jesus' example in crying? in not crying?

Our Family Prayers

One thing people do when they see someone cry is give that person a hug. So blob together, really close, for a family hug and prayer time. As you scrunch together in your family prayer hug, have each family member pray whatever is on his or her mind about crying. Maybe it's asking God to help them cry once in a while without feeling embarrassed about it, or maybe it's praying about a situation that brings tears to their eyes. Then have someone close by thanking God for the gift of tears and for Jesus' perfect example of when it's OK to cry.

(You can reuse the tissues by putting them in a bag for later use or by creating a decorative tissue bouquet to set on the table as a reminder of God's gift of tears.)

During the Week

Whenever you reach for or see someone use a tissue...

• talk about something that creates strong feelings within you. It could be something going on in your family right now or something tragic in the news that touches you.

• sneak up behind a family member, and give that person a surprise hug—just for the fun of it!

To remind you that sometimes it's OK to cry, memorize the shortest verse in the Bible, John 11:35.

---

it's a two-way street

TALK TOPIC: *Patience*

Our Family Stories

Have you ever gritted your teeth and sneered, "I'm starting to lose my patience with you!"? Grrr... No matter how hard we fight it, we all lose patience at some time or another.

Think about all the things that happen each day that cause people to lose their patience. Have one person volunteer to be the family scribe and write down all the times you think of. But put a twist on the list. Have each person "become" a different family member for a few minutes and tell what tries that person's patience in the family. Parents can become the children, or children can become their siblings—you get the gist. Have fun creating your impatience list!

Finished? Does anything surprise you? How well do you know what makes each other impatient? What does the list reveal about what makes your family lose patience?

Today's Memory Maker

It's easiest to be patient when others don't do things that might cause us to become frustrated and lose our cool. Try this little experiment to see exactly how this works.

Place two bowls and one teaspoon on a table. Fill one bowl with water. Then have the family member whose birthday is farthest from today (the one who needs to be most patient to wait for birthday presents!) take the teaspoon and begin filling the empty bowl with water, spoonful by spoonful.

As the person fills the bowl, have everyone else say things that really bug them when someone is impatient with them. For example, they might say, "Hurry up!" "What's wrong with you?" or "Why can't you do it right the first time?"

When you run out of things to say, talk about how this is like what happens when family members become impatient with each other. How is this different? How did the person filling the bowl feel while this was going on? How does getting impatient help the situation? make things harder?

Now have the person fill the empty bowl simply by pouring the water from one bowl to the next. Do others have time to bug the "pourer"? Why or why not? How might family members help each other keep their patience by doing things faster?

Today's Bible Insight

Look up 1 Corinthians 13, the famous "Love Chapter," and read the first half of verse 4: "Love is patient and kind." Patience and kindness go hand in hand. How might the atmosphere around your house change if each one of you were more patient? if each were kinder?

The water experiment demonstrated that patience is a two-way street. Both people involved have a part to play in making the world a more patient one.

So put your family scribe back to work. Have this person write, "Love is patient and kind" at the top of your impatience list. Then analyze the list from two perspectives. First, ask what each person can do to improve the situation. For example, if you wrote, "Kim is never ready to leave when we need to go somewhere," brainstorm what Kim could do to get ready on time. She might decide what to wear the night before or get ready before doing something else that seems more fun. Then write what the other family members need to do to help the situation. Is it not yelling or picking on Kim? Is it working with Kim to get out of the house?

For each "impatient" episode, see how the two-way street works. Help each other think up ways to make the family work together in love, patience, and kindness.

Our Family Prayers

Gather around the two bowls and the teaspoon for an eye-open prayer. To begin, have family members each drop a spoonful of water into the empty bowl as they ask God's help for patience in specific areas. For example, family members might pray for the ability to overlook something little that annoys them or the patience to count to ten when they feel like blowing up.

Then conclude by having one person pour the rest of the water into the bowl while he or she thanks God for overflowing with patience toward us.

During the Week

Every time you see a bowl and spoon...

• apologize to family members with whom you've lost your patience or whom you've caused to lose patience with you.

• thank a family member for being patient with you. At the end of the week, celebrate your "patience progress" with a bowl of ice cream.

To help you remember 1 Corinthians 13:4a, work together to come up with creative rhymes of the words: "Love is patient and kind." Maybe you can even create a family rap! How about using spoons to click out a rhythm? Here's an example to get your creative juices flowing:

Love is patient.
Love is kind.
God's great love
Is on my mind!

more than puppy love

TALK TOPIC: *God's love*

Our Family Stories

Lots of families have pets they love. Some people even think of their pets as members of the family. This shouldn't be too surprising because God gave us the responsibility to care for animals. (Check out Genesis 1:20-28 for more details.)

Take a moment for each family member to tell a pet story. It could be about a special pet that died, a funny story about a current pet, or

even a wish-we-had-a-pet story. After everyone's had a chance to tell a story, discuss why you think God provided humans with pets and what we can learn from taking care of them.

Today's Memory Maker

This memory maker is a little different from others. It involves your family pet. If you don't have a pet, pretend that you do or think about a pet of someone you know. You might even use your favorite stuffed animal to be a stand-in pet!

Imagine your pet could talk. What do you think it would say? Take turns telling what you think your pet would say about your family. What is your pet's favorite food? game? What does your pet appreciate most about each person? What does your pet like least? What would your pet say if you stopped caring for it? How does your pet know that you love it?

Today's Bible Insight

The Bible often uses "picture images" to help us understand more about God. One picture image compares God to a shepherd and us to his sheep. Just as we love and take care of our pets, God loves and takes care of us. But we're much more valuable to God than any pet could ever be! Have one person read John 10:11-15, where Jesus talks about himself as the good shepherd.

Stop and think about that for a moment, then discuss the following questions:

• How is your relationship with your pet like God's relationship with you? How is it different?

• What's hardest about taking care of a pet? What do you think is God's greatest difficulty with us?

• Would you give your life for your pet? Why or why not? Why did Jesus give his life for us?

• In what specific ways can we tell God thank you for his love during the coming week?

Our Family Prayers

Another Scripture passage that talks about God as a shepherd is

Psalm 23. To conclude your devotion, use a fill-in-the-name version of Psalm 23 as each person's special prayer. Join hands, and then have one person read Psalm 23, substituting each family member's name wherever the psalmist uses the words "me," "my," or "I." Make sure the reader is included in the prayer, too.

During the Week

Every time you see your pet or someone else's pet...

- thank God for the love he showed in Jesus as well as for the love of family and pets.
- have fun with an animal—you might even go to a petting zoo or an animal shelter!

Work together as a family to learn Psalm 23. For example, you might create a poster of a shepherd and sheep, then write the words to the psalm on the poster. The psalm can comfort you in every situation. Pray it often.

i just don't fit in!

TALK TOPIC: *Embarrassment*

Our Family Stories

I don't know when we started this tradition, but maybe your family will enjoy it, too. We love to hear about each other's embarrassing moments. Like the time I barged into the men's restroom thinking it was the stairway! Oops!

So don't be embarrassed. Tell each other about embarrassing moments you've had. Vote to see who has the funniest incident. By the way, time has a great way of helping us laugh about things that may have seemed unbearably horrible when they happened, but remember to laugh *with* each other, not *at* each other.

After you've all shared what made you blush, talk about what makes something embarrassing. Why is one thing embarrassing to one person and not to another? What have you learned about each other from your stories?

Today's Memory Maker

Have everyone take a close look at the illustration of the cup in the margin. Without revealing your answers, have each person decide whether or not the circle will fit on the table.

When everyone has decided, find out who is correct. Have someone take a thin piece of paper, trace the circle, cut it out, and place it on the table in the illustration. Well, how does it fit?

Then talk about what you can learn from this optical illusion. Why doesn't the circle fit even though it looks as if it would? When have you felt that you don't "fit"? Why does not fitting into a situation cause us to feel embarrassed? How do you feel when you don't fit into a situation?

Today's Bible Insight

No matter how much we may feel that we don't fit in or that we're all alone, Jesus is always with us. Right before Jesus went back to heaven, he let his disciples in on a big promise. Read Matthew 28:20b to discover what that promise is.

Think about it. Jesus is always with us. Even when we're completely embarrassed, Jesus isn't embarrassed to be with us. But are we embarrassed to have Jesus with us? Take a few minutes to discuss the following questions:

• How can knowing that Jesus is with you help you not to be embarrassed about not fitting in?

• When are you glad Jesus is with you? When are you embarrassed that Jesus is with you?

• How can knowing that Jesus is with you help you not be embarrassed about being a Christian?

- How can we help each other get over embarrassing moments? not be embarrassed about Jesus?

Our Family Prayers

Form a standing circle, and hold hands. Begin with the person wearing the most red (the color most often associated with embarrassment). Have that person say a brief prayer for the family member to the right, asking God to help him or her not be embarrassed, especially about knowing Jesus. Continue around the family circle until everyone has prayed.

During the Week

Every time you see something that's bright red...
- be on the lookout for ways to befriend someone in an embarrassing moment.
- give a family member a high five, and remind that person Jesus is always with us!

At least once a day, tell each other about your embarrassing moments that day. Make sure you support one another with lots of love and laughter. Then, when you're done telling your stories, say Matthew 28:20b together as a reminder that Jesus is never embarrassed to be with us!

nobody likes me!

TALK TOPIC: *Hurt feelings*

Our Family Stories

Ever had one of those days when you feel as though everyone's out to get you? The world just launched a campaign against you, nobody likes you, and life is the pits.

Let every family member describe a time he or she felt just plain yucky. Each person can complete this sentence: "The last time I felt nobody liked me and everyone was out to get me was..." But before you start, set some ground rules. Listen with your hearts. While each person talks, keep an encouraging atmosphere going. This isn't the time to make jokes or wisecracks.

When you're done, talk about anything you learned about each other. How are your stories alike? How are they different? How often do members of your family feel this way?

Today's Memory Maker

Before the devotion, have one family member volunteer to create two look-alike piles of sugar and salt. You need only about a teaspoon of each. It's important that no one else knows which is which.

Present the two piles to the rest of the family. Then have each person silently guess which pile is the sugar. When everyone has guessed, have the rest of the family close their eyes as one by one each family member taste tests his or her guess. Gulp!

When everyone is finished, discuss what just happened. How did you feel if you got it right? if you guessed wrong? How is this like guessing what someone is feeling on the inside? How do you know when a family member is hurting? feeling good? Can you always tell what someone is feeling on the inside? Why or why not?

Today's Bible Insight

We can get pretty good at hiding what's going on inside of us—especially if it's yucky stuff we don't want anybody else to know. It's a lot like pretending to be sugar when we're really salt. But God always knows the truth about what's going on inside us. Take a careful look at Psalm 139:1-12 to learn what God's Word says about this.

Then answer the following questions to see how this applies to your family:

- Why do you think we can't hide anything from God?
- Why do we sometimes want to hide things from God?
- Why do we sometimes try to hide things from our families?

Sometimes we think people wouldn't love us if they knew everything about us. But God loves us—and he knows everything about us! That's called unconditional love—love with no strings attached. That's exactly the kind of love God wants us to show each other. So take turns listing ways you can show this love to a family member who's hurting. For example, you might spend time with someone who's feeling lonely or promise to apologize to someone whose feelings you hurt. To help you follow through with your ideas, write them on a sheet of paper, and hang it on the refrigerator door or in another prominent place.

Our Family Prayers

Form a close standing circle. One by one, have each family member place one hand in the center of your family, palm up, ready to receive your family's love prayers. Then take turns adding a second hand to the pile as family members each ask God to help them be sensitive and loving to that person when he or she is feeling unloved.

During the Week

Every time you see a container of sugar or salt...

• ask the family member nearest you whether he or she feels sweet or salty and why. Listen, then tell and show that family member you love him or her.

• ask yourself if you are trying to hide something from anyone. If so, pray about what God wants you to do about that.

Whenever someone asks for salt or sugar at the table, have the entire family say Psalm 139:1 before you pass it to him or her.

I wish...

TALK TOPIC: *Hopes and dreams*

Our Family Stories

Everyone has hopes and dreams for the future. Kids dream of the day they're old enough to stay up past 9 p.m. or go to the store alone. Parents hope for new houses, job promotions, or even a few minutes of peace and quiet at the end of each day.

What about your family's hopes for the future? Have family members each tell what they hope will happen to them during the next week, the next month, and the next year. The answers could range from learning to use the computer to making the team to getting a new job. What hopes do you have for yourselves?

Today's Memory Maker

Most of us go on day to day without ever thinking about our hopes for our families. Here's your chance to remedy that. For the next few minutes (or however long you want to take), make a list of what you each want most for your family. Make it your ultimate "family wish list." Let the person in the family who really likes to make lists be the recorder.

Make sure everyone contributes because each person is an important member of the family! To do this, have each person complete the following sentence: "What I wish most for our family is..." Some ideas might include more time together, a bigger house, or that everyone will get along better. Be sure that these "family" wishes really are for the family and not just for the person making the wish.

When you're done listing wishes, discuss what the list reveals about your family. How easy was it to agree on your family wishes? How are these wishes like your wishes for yourselves? How are they different? What does the list reveal about what is important to your family? What do you think God wishes for your family?

Then together decide a special place to keep the family wish list. Maybe you'll lock it in a safe, put it on the refrigerator, or stash it in a desk drawer—you decide.

Today's Bible Insight

Your family is part of an even greater family—the family of God, and God has some pretty big wishes for all of us. Find John 17:17-21 in your Bible, and have one person read what Jesus prayed not long before he was crucified. It's Jesus' family wish list for his followers.

Jesus is praying for your family! Discuss the following questions to see exactly what Jesus wishes for your family:
- What exactly does Jesus wish for our family?
- How do you feel about Jesus' wishes for us?

• How well are we meeting Jesus' hopes for us?
• What can we do to meet Jesus' wishes better?

Then compare your family wish list to Jesus' hopes for your family. If necessary, revise your family wish list so it better matches Jesus' wishes for your family. You want to make sure that everything you're wishing for is something Jesus wishes for your family, too.

Our Family Prayers

Have one person read one wish listed on the family wish list. Then have someone else pray that God will help you work toward achieving that wish or show you how it needs to be changed. Take turns reading and praying until you've covered the entire list. Amen!

During the Week

Every time you see your family wish list...

• ask the family member nearest you if there are any new wishes to add to the list.

• work together as a family to develop a plan to work toward meeting one or more wishes.

To remind you that Jesus wishes us all to serve, every time someone points to the family wish list, recite John 17:17 together: "Make them ready for your service through your truth; your teaching is truth." Then name one thing you did today that served God.

---

consider the ant

TALK TOPIC: *Chores*

Our Family Stories

One thing about being a family is that each person plays an important role in the family "chore chain." Maybe you've heard of a food chain. Well, families operate with a chore chain! That simply means that each person has a valuable role in making family life really work.

What about your family's chore chain? List on a piece of paper every chore in your family and who's responsible for that chore. Make your list as complete as possible—no chore is too small to be included. Then decide which chores you think are most important, which are least important, and why.

Today's Memory Maker

Take a look at the ant in the picture. How much weight do you think this little creature can carry? Did you know that a leaf ant can carry ten times its body weight? That's pretty impressive! Do you think you could lift something that weighs ten times as much as you do? Figure out how heavy a load that would be—then give it a try!

Now create a family "sign" to represent a hard worker. For example, you might show your arm muscles like a champion wrestler. Then give each other the sign for a hard worker!

Funny thing about ants. They live in colonies in which every ant has a special job. They're organized in such a way that they can't exist without each other. How is your family like an ant colony? How organized is your family chore chain? How well is your chore chain working?

Now take a look at the sloth. Sloths don't do much of anything. They are the opposite of ants. In fact, sloths only leave their restful tree limbs once a week to go to the bathroom. They spend their entire lives hanging from a tree, moving only enough to feed themselves. Think up a sign to represent a lazy worker. You might show three center fingers on each hand to represent the three-toed sloth. Then give each other the sign for lazy worker.

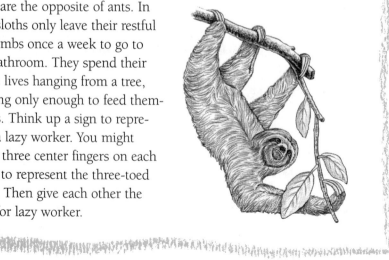

Sometimes animals mirror the way humans act. How is your family's attitude toward chores like that of a sloth? How is it different? Why do people sometimes feel slothful about chores?

Now have a volunteer read through your family chore list one by one. After each chore is read, have family members each give the hard worker or the lazy worker sign to represent how he or she feels about that chore. What does this reveal about your family's feelings about chores? Are you more like hard-working ants or lazy sloths? Explain. How do you think God wants us to do our chores?

Today's Bible Insight

Open your Bible, and read Colossians 3:23, a verse that was written for workers. Then discuss the following questions:

• Does God want us to work more like ants or like sloths? Explain.

• When is it tempting not to do our best when we're doing chores?

• How can knowing that we're working for God help us do our best?

• How can we remind each other to work hard when we do chores?

Colossians puts a whole new spin on who we're working for. So have each person name one thing he or she can start doing immediately to work for God—and not for people.

Our Family Prayers

To close, have each person tell whether he or she works more like an ant or a sloth and why. Then have everyone say a personal prayer out loud for God's guidance in his or her attitude toward your family chore chain.

During the Week

Be on the lookout for creatures that can teach you a lesson about work. Every time you spot one...

- thank God that you have the privilege of working for the Lord of the universe.
- "work" at memorizing Colossians 3:23—recite it every time you're doing a chore.

For extra fun, have the artistic members of your family draw or trace pictures of the ant. Then give an ant picture to a family member as a thank you for a chore well done.

who's in control?

TALK TOPIC: *Holy Spirit*

Our Family Stories

Who doesn't like the feeling of power and control? Parents wish they could control their kids, and kids want to be in charge of themselves. Do you think everyone in your family has had times they felt they were in control or in charge?

Give each person the spotlight for a few moments to tell about a time that he or she felt in complete control. How did this make that person feel? For example, Mom might have felt in control when she finally got all the kids buckled into their seats and ready to go. One of the kids might have felt in charge when he or she was able to choose the game for recess.

Take time to hear each person's story. Then discuss what it's like to be in control of people or situations. What do you like about being in control? What's scary about being in control? What do you like about someone else being in control of you? What don't you like about that?

Today's Memory Maker

Simon Says is a great game to learn about being in control and being controlled. So spend some time playing Simon Says as a family. You'll have the most fun (and also learn the most!) if Simon has everyone else do wacky actions, such as bark like a dog, waddle like a duck, or make a goofy face.

Make sure that everyone—no matter how young or old—leads at least one game. That way everyone will know how it feels to control others and to be controlled by others.

After you're done playing, discuss what you liked and didn't like about the game. How did you feel when you were leading the game? How did you feel when someone else was leading? How is this game like trying to control your own life? How is it different? How is it like giving control of your life to God? How is it different?

Today's Bible Insight

God always wants what's best for us—including giving control of our lives to him. Read Romans 8:5-6 to learn why it's smart to put God's Spirit in charge of our lives. Then discuss the following questions:

• Why does God want us to be controlled by the Holy Spirit?
• When is it hard to give control of our lives to God's Spirit?
• How can we make it easier to give control to God's Spirit?

Then, to help you apply this truth to your everyday lives, make a chart like the one on page 102. List on the left side of the chart at least one challenge or problem that each person will face during the next week. For example, you might list a big test at school, a difficult work project, a busy schedule, or an unkind neighbor. Make two columns to the right of the list. Label the first column "If I'm in charge" and the second "If God's Spirit is in charge."

	If I'm in charge	If God's Spirit is in charge
Big test at school		
Difficult project at work		
Busy schedule		
Unkind neighbor		

After you've created your chart, talk about each problem or challenge, and describe how you might be tempted to control the situation and how you could give control of the situation to God. Then talk about why it would be best to let God's Spirit be in control of these situations.

Our Family Prayers

Gather around the chart you just created. Have everyone choose one challenge or problem that another family member will be facing during the next week. Then take turns praying for the Holy Spirit's guiding and leading in that area. Then hang your chart in a prominent location to remind you to give control of your life to God. At the end of the week, you can also evaluate how well you gave control of that situation to God.

During the Week

Every time you see your chart...

• ask a family member how well he or she is giving control of the listed situation to God.

• gather everyone to play a game of Simon Says—be sure each person gets a chance to lead!

To remind you to give control of your lives to God, write out Romans 8:5 on another chart, and read it aloud several times during the week.

listen up!

TALK TOPIC: *Listening*

Our Family Stories

Listening is an important ingredient of good communication. When family members listen to each other, they're less likely to misunderstand or quarrel with one another.

So take some time to listen to each other. Have each person complete the following sentence: "The time I felt most listened to in our family was..." Make sure everyone explains why he or she felt listened to. Then have each person complete this sentence: "The time I felt least listened to in our family was..." When everyone has finished both sentences, talk about what surprised you about each other's answers. What things make you feel listened to? What makes you feel you're not being listened to?

Today's Memory Maker

Here's a fun listening experiment to do together. Have a volunteer sit in a chair with his or her eyes closed. Then have someone else stand beside the volunteer, hold his or her hand about a foot above the volunteer's head, and snap his or her fingers. (This person can also clap.) Then the volunteer has to guess which side the sound is

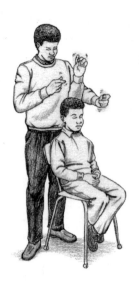

coming from. This works best when the sound maker snaps or claps over and around the person's head in an equal distance between both ears of the listener. That way it's harder to tell where the sound is coming from.

When the sound is exactly between both ears, your ears can fool you—that's what makes this experiment so much fun. Even the youngest of family members will enjoy fooling the listener. Take turns having family members be the listeners and the snappers. When everyone has had a turn, talk about how this experiment is like listening in real life.

How is this game like what happens when we try to listen to each other? How is it different? Why do we sometimes not hear what another family member is trying to tell us? What happens when we don't hear each other accurately?

Today's Bible Insight

God knows it isn't easy to communicate. It takes hard work. And it all begins with listening. You've probably heard that God gave us two ears and one mouth for a reason!

So open your Bible to James 1:22-25, and have everyone listen carefully to the words as a volunteer reads them. Then discuss what God's Word can teach us about listening to each other.

- How do these verses describe truly listening to someone?
- Why is it important to listen to God? to do what God says?
- Why is it important for families to listen to one another?

Now list all the practical ways your family members can become better listeners. For example, you might decide to look at the person who's talking, to turn off the television when someone wants to talk to you, or to put down the newspaper when someone is speaking.

Our Family Prayers

To put what you learned about listening into practice, take turns telling what your prayer needs are right now. Make sure that other family members listen carefully. Then pray for that person's needs. Continue until each person has been prayed for.

During the Week

Every time someone snaps his or her fingers...

• recite James 1:22 together—you might even snap your fingers and say the verse in rhythm!

• grab a chair, and play several rounds of the game in "Today's Memory Maker" together.

To help you remember both to listen carefully and to act on what you hear, use "snapping fingers" as your secret family code for "Listen up!"

lean on me

TALK TOPIC: *God's help*

Our Family Stories

Every family has to face tough times. For some it's the loss of a job and not enough money to buy food and clothes. Maybe it's been a scary illness, a broken marriage, or a big move away from family and friends. Every family goes through hard times, but God placed us in families to help us deal with them.

What have been the hardest things for your family? Although it may not be easy, have each family member tell what has been the scariest or most difficult time in his or her life. What made that time so hard? Did you feel all alone? helpless? afraid? What gave you the strength to get through that hard time? How did your family help you get through that time?

Today's Memory Maker

Now try this experiment to discover where the strength to get through hard times really comes from. Choose one family member (age or size won't matter), and have that person lean against a wall, place both palms on the wall, and lock his or her arms. Then have the person place one foot forward and one foot back so it looks as though that person is boldly holding up the wall.

Now have the rest of the family line up behind the first person and gently push against the shoulders of the family member in front of him or her. Can you budge the person pushing against the wall? If you're doing the experiment correctly, no number of people will be able to move that person! For fun, try it with different wall pushers!

Once everyone has had a turn, talk about what surprised you about the activity. Why were you unable to budge the person pushing against the wall? What if the first person hadn't been supported with the wall? What supports us when we're going through tough times? What if we don't have supports during those times?

Today's Bible Insight

God doesn't want us to fall when we're going through tough times, so he provided supports that will help us stand. Open your Bible to Psalm 46:1, and read this verse to discover what those supports are.

One Bible translates this verse: "God is our protection and our strength. He always helps in times of trouble." Talk about what the words "protection" and "strength" mean to your family.

• How has God protected our family during times of trouble?
• How can God use us to protect each other during hard times?
• How has God's strength "held us up" during difficult times?
• How can God use us to hold each other up during hard times?

Now list some of the tough situations your family is facing right now. Then talk about how God can protect and strengthen you during this time. Be sure you also talk about how you can protect and strengthen each other at this time. Remember the lesson of "Today's Memory Maker"—you must lean on God *and* on each other to get through tough times.

Our Family Prayers

To close, hold hands really tightly—not enough to hurt, but enough to show strength. Have everyone thank God for protecting and strengthening your family in the past and ask God to help your family through tough times in the future. Then conclude with a hefty, loving family hug.

During the Week

Watch for unusual walls this week. When you notice a unique quality in a wall...

• tell the family member nearest you how that quality is like or unlike God's strength and protection.

• gather several people to do the "wall experiment"—remember to give God the credit for being our help.

To reinforce the lesson of this devotion, create a poster or a decorative wall hanging with Psalm 46:1 on it.

just for the fun of it!

TALK TOPIC: *Laughter*

Our Family Stories

My family just likes to have fun! We love the times we laugh so hard that we snort or cry or feel just plain silly. Every day we watch for funny and fun things in life that bring us a smile.

What does your family like to do "just for the fun of it"? Is it biking together? Is it making microwave popcorn and root beer floats on Saturday nights? Is it seeing who can make the silliest face? What do you do together for fun? The key words here are "TOGETHER" and "FUN." So take turns telling the "funniest" or "funnest" times you remember having with your family. Ready? Set? Ho! (Or is it "ha"?) Go!

Today's Memory Maker

Now take some time to do something really goofy and fun. Everyone will need to lie down on the floor—a soft rug or carpet will work best!—to create a human zigzag. Have one person lie down on his or her back. Then have someone else lie down with his or her head on that person's stomach. Repeat this until everyone in the family has his or her head on someone's stomach—except the first person, of course!

Now have the first person say, "Ha!" (This game takes belly laughs to new heights!) Then the second person in the zigzag should say, "Ha! Ha!" and the third person, "Ha! Ha! Ha!" and so on. Each person should add one more "ha" to the silliness. The only catch is that you all must try *not* to laugh. Keep adding "ha's" until someone really can't stop laughing.

After you've played several times, sit together in a circle and discuss what you liked about this game. What about it was fun? What wasn't fun? What makes something fun to do? What makes something not fun? When do you as a family have fun together? Do you think your family has enough fun together? Why or why not?

Today's Bible Insight

Sometimes people think that God wants us always to be solemn and serious, but that's simply not true. Look up and read Philippians 4:4 to find out how God wants us to act. A popular praise song even uses the words to this verse: "Rejoice in the Lord always, and again I say, rejoice!" If you know that song, go ahead and sing it!

Then take a few minutes to discuss the following questions:
- What does it mean to "rejoice in the Lord always"?
- How are rejoicing and having fun alike? different?
- Do you think Jesus laughed much? Why or why not?
- What things keep us from rejoicing? from having fun?

Then have each person list one thing that would be fun to do together as a family during the coming week. Record everyone's idea, and then begin to make plans to do that fun thing. (You may even want to start planning a fun family outing or vacation!)

Our Family Prayers

Just for the fun of it—hold pinkies instead of hands! Then have family members each thank God for one thing that brings them joy because they're a part of your family. Conclude by giving each other (and God!) a big smile and a heartfelt laugh.

During the Week

Every time you see something funny...
- thank God for the gift of laughter, smiles, and joy—then share that gift with a family member!
- make sure that it isn't something that would hurt someone or make that person feel laughed at.

To help you all learn Philippians 4:4, sing, "Rejoice in the Lord always, and again I say, rejoice" together. As the week goes on, see if you can sing it in a round!

God's road signs

TALK TOPIC: *Right and wrong*

Our Family Stories

Our world is filled with all kinds of signs. Signs tell us which direction to turn, which room we're supposed to go in, and when to walk or not walk. Some signs say "Do Not Enter," while others tell us to go or to stop. Life would be confusing if we didn't have signs to help us find our way.

Take a few minutes to tell about times you got lost or made a mistake because you didn't follow a sign. Maybe you wandered into the wrong room at school or got lost on the family vacation. What-ever it is, tell how you got lost, what happened after you got lost, and how you corrected your mistake. Then discuss how you felt when you missed or misread the sign. What did you learn from this experience?

Today's Memory Maker

For the next few moments, play a fun game to learn more about how we all need help knowing where to go. Form pairs and have one partner close his or her eyes. Have the "eye-open" partner spin the first person around and then lead the closed-eye partner around the house. Have the leading partner guide the following partner by telling him or her to step forward, turn to the right, and so on. This game works best if leaders don't physically guide their followers—except, of course, to keep them from getting hurt.

Have leaders guide their partners through an obstacle course that takes them around chairs, down halls, and up stairs. Make sure leaders don't take their followers anywhere unsafe—you don't want any-one to get hurt. After the followers complete the obstacle course, have partners change places and repeat the game.

Then come back together and talk about your game. How did it feel to lead someone? to be led? When you were following, how did you know you were being led in the right direction? When you were leading, how did you make sure your partner didn't get hurt? How is this game like following signs in real life? How is it different?

Today's Bible Insight

Life is full of decisions about what's right and what's wrong. God wants us to make wise choices so we always stay on the right road. But where can we find the signs that tell us which road to take? Find and read Proverbs 4:25-27 to find out the answer to this question. Then discuss the following questions to apply these verses to your day-to-day lives:

- How can we know whether something is right or wrong?
- Where can we look to find out where God wants us to go?
- What should we do if we don't know the right way to go?
- What will happen if we go the wrong way? the right way?

Now have family members each think of a situation they often face in which they need to choose between right and wrong. For example, one person might be tempted to join in gossip about a co-worker; someone else might be in a group of friends who are making fun of someone different. Then discuss each situation and help each other list what God says to do in situations like that, what might happen if the person chose the wrong way, and what might happen if he or she chose the right way. As much as possible, help each other understand what the right "path" is in each situation and why it's wisest to follow that path.

Our Family Prayers

Join hands and have family members pray for their partners from the earlier game. Ask God to help each family member make the right decisions in the situations you discussed earlier.

During the Week

Every time you see any kind of sign...

• tell a family member how God might use that sign to help you make a good decision.

• point toward the sign and say Proverbs 4:27 with the family member nearest you.

For extra fun, decorate your home with signs. To remind you to follow the direction of God's Word, cut out sign shapes and then write on them the words from Proverbs 4:25-27.

Topical Index